The
Bite-Sized Book of

Trivia

The
Bite-Sized Book of

Trivia

T. J. M^cTAVISH

GIFT BOOKS.

THOMAS NELSON PUBLISHERS
Since 1798

Produced with the assistance of The Livingstone Corporation (www.LivingstoneCorporation.com). Project staff includes Don Jones, Phoebe Blaustein, Andy Culbertson, Mark Pool, Ashley Taylor, and Dave Veerman.

ISBN 978-1-59530-012-6
BOK5543

Printed and bound in China

PREFACE

This book is for those of you who actually enjoy the minutiae of life—the arcane details that others simply overlook. It is full of conversation pieces, oddities, and knickknacks, every one of which is drawn from my favorite book, the Bible. (Apparently, it's a lot of people's favorite, being the best-selling book of all time).

I'd warn you about the danger of wasting precious hours poring over these little trinkets of knowledge and fact, but apparently you didn't listen. So don't blame me if you get caught up in this and find yourself neglecting the more important things in life—like food . . . water . . . sleep . . . and television.

Enjoy.

T.J. McTavish

❄ MAJOR THEMES IN THE BIBLE ❄

- **God:** "Oh, the depth of the riches of the wisdom and knowledge of God! / How unsearchable his judgments, / and his paths beyond tracing out! / Who has known the mind of the Lord? / Or who has been his counselor? / Who has ever given to God, / that God should repay him? / For from him and through him and to him are all things" (Rom. 11:33–36).
- **Creation:** "In the beginning God created the heavens and the earth" (Gen. 1:1).
- **Humanity:** "So God created man in his own image, / in the image of God he created him; / male and female he created them" (Gen. 1:27).

- **Sin:** "For all have sinned and fall short of the glory of God" (Rom. 3:23).
- **Judgment:** "For the wages of sin is death" (Rom. 6:23).
- **Redemption:** "God was reconciling the world to himself in Christ" (2 Cor. 5:19).
- **Faith:** "Without faith it is impossible to please God" (Heb. 11:6).
- **Love:** "Greater love has no one than this, that he lay down his life for his friends" (John 15:13).
- **Immortality:** "Where, O death, is your victory? / Where, O death, is your sting?" (1 Cor. 15:55).

❄ MIRACULOUS BIRTHS ❄

The fact that Christ's earthly mother had not had sexual relations prior to her first-born's birth qualifies Jesus's arrival on earth as unique and supernatural. But in the Bible many women who, because of infertility or old age, should not have been physically capable of having children did so miraculously:

- Isaac was born to Sarah and Abraham (Gen. 21:2).
- Esau and Jacob were born to Rebekah and Isaac (Gen. 25:21).
- Joseph was born to Rachel and Jacob (Gen. 30:22–23).
- Samson was born to Manoah and his unnamed wife (Judg. 13:3).
- Samuel was born to Elkanah and Hannah (1 Sam. 1:20).
- John the Baptist was born to Elizabeth and Zechariah (Luke 1:24–25).

❄ MEN AND WOMEN OF THE BIBLE WITH TWO NAMES ❄

Judas Iscariot • Simon Peter • Mary Magdalene • Jesus Christ •
Pontius Pilate • Bar-Jesus • John Mark • Herod Antipas

❄ PLAGUES AND THEIR OCCASIONS ❄

Although today we tend to think of plagues as devastating infectious diseases, the Bible uses the term in a broader sense. As you will note below, some plagues affect nature directly (darkness, hail) or cause an outbreak of destructive natural effects (gnats, flies, locusts). Various examples from Scripture demonstrate that God has used such events as instruments of judgment. Consider:

Plague	Scripture Reference	Occasion
Water turned to blood	Exodus 7:20	When Pharaoh would not release the Israelites.
Frogs	Exodus 8:6	When Pharaoh would not release the Israelites.
Flies	Exodus 8:24	When Pharaoh would not release the Israelites.
Hail	Exodus 9:24	When Pharaoh would not release the Israelites.
Darkness	Exodus 10:22	When Pharaoh would not release the Israelites.
Death of firstborn in Egypt	Exodus 12:29	When Pharaoh would not release the Israelites.
Death of three thousand Israelites by sword	Exodus 32:27	When the Israelites worshiped false gods.
Death of Israelites by fire	Numbers 11:1	When the Israelites complained to God.
Poisonous snakes	Numbers 21:6	God allowed deadly bites in judgment for rebellion.
Death by a mysterious plague	Numbers 11:31–34	When the Israelites complained to God.
Earthquake	Numbers 16:32	God killed the Israelites for rebellion.
Tumors	1 Samuel 5:8–9	God's judgment on Philistia for capturing the ark of God.
Death	1 Samuel 6:19	God claimed the lives of those who looked in the ark of God.
Death	2 Samuel 24:15	God's judgment when King David took a census.
Blindness	2 Kings 6:18	When the Arameans attacked Israel.

Plague	Scripture Reference	Occasion
Leprosy	Numbers 12:1–10	When Miriam and Aaron criticized Moses
Paralysis	1 Kings 13:4	God judged Jeroboam's false religion
Eaten alive by worms	Acts 12:20–23	When King Herod accepted worship

❀ FAMOUS (AND-NOT-SO FAMOUS) SHEPHERDS ❀

When you think of shepherds in the Bible, you tend to think of those who are associated with the original cast of Christmas. And those in Luke 2 definitely count. But they aren't the only shepherds in Scripture. Consider:

- Abel, the first family's sheep keeper (Gen. 4:2).
- Abraham owned a lot of sheep and oxen (Gen. 12:16).
- Lot, Abraham's nephew, chose to graze his livestock in Sodom (Gen. 13:5).
- Isaac carried on the family business his father, Abraham, began (Gen. 26:14).
- Jacob went to work for his uncle Laban as a shepherd and then established his own flocks (Gen. 30:32).
- Laban, Jacob's uncle and Rachel's father, was a shepherd before turning the flocks over to his nephew (Gen. 31:19).
- Joseph was charged with caring for the sheep of his father, Jacob (Gen. 37:2).
- Judah, the fourth son of Jacob, and Joseph's older brother, tended sheep (Gen. 38:12).
- Reuel, the father-in-law of Moses, had extensive flocks. He's also called Jethro (Exod. 2:16).
- Moses was tending sheep when God spoke to him in the burning bush (Exod. 3:1).
- David, Israel's greatest king, first worked for his dad watching the family flock (1 Sam. 16:11).
- Nabal, an unkind shepherd who insulted David (1 Sam. 25:2).
- Amos, a shepherd God called to become a prophet (Amos 7:15).
- Jesus called himself "the good shepherd" (John 10:11).
- Peter was called by Jesus to be a shepherd of those who followed God (John 21:15).

❋ MUSICAL INSTRUMENTS MENTIONED IN THE BIBLE ❋

Flute . . . . Genesis 4:21
Harp . . . . 1 Samuel 10:5
Tambourines . . . . Genesis 31:27
Lyres . . . . 1 Chronicles 16:5
Cymbals . . . . Psalm 150:5
Trumpet . . . . 2 Samuel 6:15
Cornet . . . . 1 Chronicles 15:28 (KJV)
Timbrel . . . . Job 21:12 (KJV)
Sackbut . . . . Daniel 3:7 (KJV)
Dulcimer . . . . Daniel 3:5 (KJV)
Viol . . . . Isaiah 14:11 (KJV)
Pipes . . . . Matthew 11:17 (KJV)
Rams' Horns . . . . Joshua 6:4
Psaltery . . . . 2 Samuel 6:5 (KJV)
Lute . . . . 1 Samuel 18:6
Organ . . . . Genesis 4:21 (KJV)

❋ WHERE DID SATAN COME FROM? ❋

Satan has not always existed. Before the creation of the universe, he was an angel whom God created. Judged because of his rebellion (which the New Testament suggests was rooted in his pride—1 Tim. 3:6), he was expelled from the presence of the Creator. Once fallen, Satan became responsible for introducing evil to this world. Simply put, Satan was given the free will as a created angel to choose whether or not he would obey God. He chose to disobey. That choice was an evil one and in the process brought evil into an otherwise perfect world.

❋ SHIELDS, SHIELDS, AND MORE SHIELDS ❋

Small shields of hammered gold (1 Kings 10:17)
Bronze shields (1 Kings 14:27)
Large shields (2 Chron. 14:8)
Rows of shields (Job 41:15)
Burning shields (Ezek. 39:9)
Oiled shields (Isa. 21:5)
Red shields (Nah. 2:3)
Large shields of hammered gold (1 Kings 10:16)

❀ INCREDIBLE JOURNEYS ❀

When people describe life as a journey, they expect that most of us will know the experiences of travel. The Bible records numerous journeys and often explains God's purposes in having individuals and nations leave one area for another. Trips are tools God uses to shape people's lives. Consider:

Itinerary	Traveler(s)	Reference
From Ur to Haran	Terah and his family	Genesis 11:31
From Haran to Canaan	Abraham and his family	Genesis 12:4–5
From Canaan to Egypt	Abraham and Sarah	Genesis 12:10–20
From Hebron to Mount Moriah	Abraham and Isaac	Genesis 22
From Nahor to Canaan	Rebekah	Genesis 24
From Beersheba to Haran	Jacob	Genesis 28–29
From Haran to Bethel	Jacob	Genesis 32–35
From Canaan to Egypt	Joseph	Genesis 37
From Canaan to Egypt	Jacob and his family	Genesis 42–46
From Egypt to Midian	Moses	Exodus 2:15
From Egypt to Canaan	The children of Israel	Exodus through Joshua
From Moab to Bethlehem	Naomi and Ruth	Ruth 1
From Africa to Jerusalem	The queen of Sheba	1 Kings 10
From Mount Carmel to Mount Horeb	Elijah	1 Kings 19
From Syria to Samaria	Naaman	2 Kings 5
From Judah to Babylon	God's people taken captive	Ezra 1; Psalm 126
From Babylon to Jerusalem	Nehemiah	Nehemiah 1–2
From Nazareth to Bethlehem	Mary and Joseph	Luke 2:4
From Persia to Bethlehem	The Magi	Matthew 2:1–12
From Bethlehem to Egypt	Mary, Joseph, and Jesus	Matthew 2:13–14
From Egypt to Nazareth	Mary, Joseph, and Jesus	Matthew 2:23
From Jerusalem to Jericho	The good Samaritan	Luke 10:25–35
From Jerusalem to Emmaus	Cleopas and his friend	Luke 24:13–35
From Samaria to the road to Gaza	Philip	Acts 8
From Jerusalem to Damascus	Paul	Acts 9
From Jerusalem to Rome	Paul	Acts 21–28
From earth to the third heaven	Paul	2 Corinthians 12:2

❦ LOVE POEMS ❦

The Bible is a one-volume library. It contains all kinds of literary styles, including historical narratives, personal journal entries, genealogical records, hymn lyrics, personal correspondence, prophecy, parables, and travelogues. One of the most poignant categories is love poetry.

The power of love between two friends
• Ecclesiastes 4:9–12

Two are better than one,
>because they have a good return for their work:

If one falls down,
>his friend can help him up. (vv. 9–10)

A woman expresses her romantic infatuation
• Song of Songs 1:2–4

Let him kiss me with the kisses of his mouth—
>for your love is more delightful than wine. (v. 2)

• Song of Songs 2:3–6

Like an apple tree among the trees of the forest
>is my lover among the young men.

I delight to sit in his shade,
>and his fruit is sweet to my taste. (v. 3)

God describes his love for the nation Israel
• Jeremiah 31:3–6

I have loved you with an everlasting love;
>I have drawn you with loving-kindness. (v. 3)

• Hosea 2:14–20

Therefore I am now going to allure her;
>I will lead her into the desert
>and speak tenderly to her. (v. 14)

• Hosea 11:1–4

When Israel was a child, I loved him,
>and out of Egypt I called my son. (v. 1)

The apostle Paul describes love among Christians
• 1 Corinthians 13:1–8

Love is patient, love is kind. It does not envy, it does not boast, it is not proud. (v. 4)

Abishag

Achan

Agabus

Ammizabad

Amram

Archippus

Berodachbaladan (KJV)

Buzi

Chushan-rishathaim (KJV)

Cozbi

Crispus

Dodavah (KJV)

Dodo

Eglon

Elmodam (KJV)

Elzabad

Epaphroditus

Eubulus

Evil-merodach

Fortunatus

Haahashtari

Hadadezer

Hammedatha

Hanani

Hashabiah

Hashupha (KJV)

Hattush

Hazar Gaddah

Hephzibah

Hizkiah

Hushah

Huzzab (KJV)

Iddo

Igdaliah

Ikkesh

Ishbi-benob (KJV)

Ish-Bosheth

Ishpan

Jahdo

Jehoshaphat

Jehudijah (KJV)

Jemimah

Jeshebeab

Jidlaph

Josabad (KJV)

Lo-Ruhamah

Machnadebai

Magor-Missabib

Magpiash

Maher-shalal-hash-baz

Mehuman

Mephibosheth

Methusaleh

Meshach

Meshelemiah

Naashon (KJV)

Nun

Orpah

Parshandatha

Philologus

Potiphar

Rabshakeh (KJV)

Regem-Melech

Ribai

Sanballat

Sennacherib

Shadrach

Shalmaneser

Shamgar

Shashak

Shelomith

Shephuphan

Syntyche

Theophilus

Tiglath-Pileser

Tohu

Tychicus

Uzzah

Vashti

Zabad

Zaphenath-Paneah

Zaza

Zebedee

Zeeb (KJV)

Zerubbabel

Ziba

Zidkijah (KJV)

Zipporah

Pharaoh . . . . Then a new king, who did not know about Joseph, came to power in Egypt. "Look," he said to his people, "the Israelites have become much too numerous for us. Come, we must deal shrewdly with them or they will become even more numerous and, if war breaks out, will join our enemies, fight against us and leave the country."

So they put slave masters over them to oppress them with forced labor, and they built Pithom and Rameses as store cities for Pharaoh. But the more they were oppressed, the more they multiplied and spread; so the Egyptians came to dread the Israelites and worked them ruthlessly. They made their lives bitter with hard labor in brick and mortar and with all kinds of work in the fields; in all their hard labor the Egyptians used them ruthlessly. . . .

Then Pharaoh gave this order to all his people: "Every boy that is born you must throw into the Nile, but let every girl live." (Exod. 1:8–14, 22)

Adoni-Zedek . . . . Now Adoni-Zedek king of Jerusalem heard that Joshua had taken Ai and totally destroyed it, doing to Ai and its king as he had done to Jericho and its king, and that the people of Gibeon had made a treaty of peace with Israel and were living near them. He and his people were very much alarmed at this, because Gibeon was an important city, like one of the royal cities; it was larger than Ai, and all its men were good fighters. So Adoni-Zedek king of Jerusalem appealed to Hoham king of Hebron, Piram king of Jarmuth, Japhia king of Lachish and Debir king of Eglon. "Come up and help me attack Gibeon," he said, "because it has made peace with Joshua and the Israelites." (Josh. 10:1–4)

Hanun . . . . In the course of time, the king of the Ammonites died, and his son Hunan succeeded him as king. David thought, "I will show kindness to Hanun son of Nahash, just as his father showed kindness to me." So David sent a delegation to express his sympathy to Hanun concerning his father.

Hanun (*cont.*) . . . . When David's men came to the land of the Ammonites, the Ammonite nobles said to Hanun their lord, "Do you think David is honoring your father by sending men to you to express sympathy? Hasn't David sent them to you to explore the city and spy it out and overthrow it?" So Hanun seized David's men, shaved off half of each man's beard, cut off their garments in the middle at the buttocks, and sent them away. (2 Sam. 10:1–4)

Jezebel . . . . Now Ahab told Jezebel everything Elijah had done and how he had killed all the prophets with the sword. So Jezebel sent a messenger to Elijah to say, "May the gods deal with me, be it ever so severely, if by this time tomorrow I do not make your life like that of one of them." Elijah was afraid and ran for his life. (1 Kings 19:1–3)

❧ ANIMALS OF THE BIBLE ❧

Ant . . . . Proverbs 6:6–7	Goat . . . . Proverbs 30:31
Ape . . . . 2 Chronicles 9:21	Hare . . . . Deuteronomy 14:7 (KJV)
Bat. . . . . Leviticus 11:19	Hornet . . . . Exodus 23:28
Bear . . . . 1 Samuel 17:34	Horse . . . . Ezra 2:66
Bee . . . . Judges 14:8	Hyena . . . . Jeremiah 50:39
Bull . . . . 1 Kings 7:25	Jackal . . . . Lamentations 4:3
Camel . . . . Ezra 2:66	Lamb . . . . Mark 14:12
Deer. . . . . Psalm 42:1	Leopard . . . . Isaiah 11:6
Dog. . . . . Proverbs 26:11	Lion . . . . Jeremiah 5:6
Donkey. . . . . Matthew 21:7	Ostrich . . . . Job 39:13–18
Dove . . . . Luke 2:24	Owl . . . . Psalm 102:6
Eagle . . . . Psalm 103:5	Partridge . . . . Jeremiah 17:11
Fish. . . . . John 21:10	Pig . . . . Matthew 7:6
Flea. . . . . 1 Samuel 24:14	Snake . . . . Amos 5:19
Fox . . . . Nehemiah 4:3	Spider . . . . Job 8:14–15
Frog. . . . . Exodus 8:2–13	Wolf . . . . Isaiah 11:6
Gnat . . . . Matthew 23:24	Worm . . . . Psalm 22:6

❈ INFAMOUS INFIDELITIES ❈

When you think of notorious romantic alliances in the Bible, your mind is quick to embrace David and Bathsheba (2 Sam. 11). But others in the Scriptures defiled the marriage bed. Consider the following:

- Leah deceived Jacob by crawling into his bed on his wedding night, pretending to be his bride (Gen. 29).
- Potiphar's wife attempted to seduce Joseph (Gen. 39).
- Hosea's wife, Gomer, was unfaithful to her husband on many occasions (Hos. 1).
- The Samaritan woman Jesus met at the well had been married five times and was currently living with a man (John 4).
- Herod had an affair with his brother's wife (Matt. 14).

❈ THE REIGNS OF THE KINGS OF JUDAH ❈

King	Reign	King	Reign
Rehoboam	930–913 BC	Jotham	750–736 BC
Abijah	913–910 BC	Ahaz	735–720 BC
Asa	910–870 BC	Hezekiah	715–699 BC
Jehoshaphat	872–847 BC	Manasseh	697–642 BC
Jehoram	848–841 BC	Amon	642–640 BC
Ahaziah	841 BC	Josiah	640–609 BC
Athaliah	841–835 BC	Jehoahaz	609 BC
Joash	835–796 BC	Jehoiakim	609–598 BC
Amaziah	796–767 BC	Jehoiachin	598 BC
Azariah	792–740 BC	Zedekiah	598–986 BC

❈ BIBLICAL BATTLE GEAR ❈

- Battering ram (Ezek. 4:2)
- Javelin (Josh. 8:18)
- Bow and arrow (2 Sam. 22:35)
- Coat of mail (1 Sam. 17:5 KJV)
- Belt with dagger (2 Sam. 20:8)
- Greaves (1 Sam. 17:6 KJV)
- Helmet (Isa. 59:17)
- Shield (1 Sam. 17:7)
- Slingshot (1 Sam. 17:40)
- Spear (Josh. 8:18 KJV)
- Sword (Gen. 27:40)
- Breastplate (Eph. 6:14)
- Stones (Acts 7:57–58)
- Rock-throwing machines (2 Chron. 26:14–15)
- Whip (John 19:1 NLT)

❧ EUPHEMISMS FOR DEATH ❧

Return to the ground (Gen. 3:19)
God took him away (Gen. 5:24)
Gathered to my people (Gen. 49:29)
Go down to the grave (1 Kings 2:6)
The silver cord is severed (Eccl. 12:6)
Fallen asleep (Acts 7:60; 1 Cor. 11:30)
Perish (John 3:16)
Gave up the ghost (Mark 15:37 KJV)

❧ THE TWELVE DISCIPLES AND ❧ THEIR PERSONALITIES

Name	Occupation	Identifiable Traits
Peter	Fisherman	Headstrong, impetuous, denied Jesus three times
John	Fisherman	Loyal, especially close to Jesus, cared for Jesus's mother, had a temper, one of the Sons of Thunder
Andrew	Fisherman	Outgoing, bold, brought his brother Peter to Jesus
Philip	Fisherman	Concerned with the nuts and bolts, Mr. Organization
James	Fisherman	Easily angered, one of the Sons of Thunder
Nathanael	Fisherman	Prejudiced, curious
Simon	Political insurrectionist	Zealous, passionate
Matthew	Tax collector	Friendly to the irreligious, hospitable
Judas Iscariot	Treasurer of the disciples	Greedy, disloyal
Thomas	Fisherman	Skeptical, prone to doubt, pessimistic
Judas son of James	Unknown	Tender-hearted, gentle
James the Less	Unknown	Patient, comfortable with being in the background

❧ HYMNS OF THE BIBLE ❧

The New Testament contains six specific references to hymns:

1. When they had sung a **hymn**, they went out to the Mount of Olives. (Matt. 26:30)

2. When they had sung a **hymn**, they went out to the Mount of Olives. (Mark 14:26)

3. About midnight Paul and Silas were praying and singing **hymns** to God, and the other prisoners were listening to them. (Acts 16:25)

4. What then, brethren? When you come together, each one has a **hymn**, a lesson, a revelation, a tongue, or an interpretation. Let all things be done for edification. (1 Cor. 14:26 RSV)

5. Addressing one another in psalms and **hymns** and spiritual songs, singing and making melody to the Lord with all your heart. (Eph. 5:19 RSV)

6. Let the word of Christ dwell in you richly, as you teach and admonish one another in all wisdom, and as you sing psalms and **hymns** and spiritual songs with thankfulness in your hearts to God. (Col. 3:16 RSV)

❧ THE FACTS OF HELL ❧

The Bible has much to say about hell. For one thing, it is referred to by several names. It is called "Sheol," "Hades," "Gehenna," and "the place of the dead" as well as "hell." New Testament writers agree that it is a place where people will be separated from the presence of a loving God. Jesus referred to it as a place of torment and of final punishment. The following verses paint a rather graphic picture:

- **Who will be there?** "But the cowardly, the unbelieving, the vile, the murderers, the sexually immoral, those who practice magic arts, the idolaters and all liars—their place will be in the fiery lake of burning sulfur. This is the second death" (Rev. 21:8).
- **Why was it created?** "The eternal fire prepared for the devil and his angels" (Matt. 25:41).
- **What will it be like?** "Where / 'their worm does not die, /and the fire is not quenched'" (Mark 9:48). "In hell, where he was in torment" (Luke 16:23).
- **Who has the power and authority to send people there?** "Fear him [God] who, after the killing of the body, has power to throw you into hell. Yes, I tell you, fear him" (Luke 12:5).

❈ ISRAEL'S REBELLION ❈

From the time Moses led the Israelites out of Egyptian bondage, they exhibited numerous evidences of their hardheartedness toward the God who delivered them.

Occasion	*Reference*
Grumbled when they saw Pharaoh's army hemming them in at the Red Sea	Exodus 14
Grumbled when they had no water	Exodus 15
Grumbled when they had no food	Exodus 16
Grumbled when they had no water	Exodus 17
Created a golden calf to worship	Exodus 32
Complained about their hardships	Numbers 11
Complained about lack of meat	Numbers 11
Rebelled against God's call to inhabit the Promised Land	Numbers 14; Deuteronomy 1
Rebelled against the Lord's command to return to the desert	Numbers 14; Deuteronomy 1
Complained about God's judgment of the 250 disobedient Levites	Numbers 16
Grumbled when they had no water	Numbers 20
Cycle of continuous rebellion: "The Israelites did evil in the sight of the LORD"	Judges 3:7 NRSV
Disregarded God's desire and insisted that they have a king like all the surrounding nations	1 Samuel 8
Jesus grieves over Israel's hardheartedness	Luke 13:34

❈ BIBLICAL BIRDS ❈

Cormorant (Lev. 11:17) • Crane (Jer. 8:7 KJV) • Cuckow
(Lev. 11:16 KJV) • Dove (Gen. 8:8 KJV) • Eagle (Jer. 49:22) • Falcon
(Deut. 14:13) • Hawk (Job 39:26) • Heron (Deut. 14:18) • Hoopoe (Lev. 11:19) •
Kite (Lev. 11:14) • Osprey (Lev. 11:18) • Ossifrage (Lev. 11:13 KJV) • Ostrich
(Job 39:13) • Owl (Isa. 34:11) • Partridge (1 Sam. 26:20) • Pelican
(Ps. 102:6 KJV) • Quail (Exod. 16:13) • Raven (Job 38:41) •
Sparrow (Matt. 10:31) • Turtledove (Gen. 15:9 KJV)

❈ "O LITTLE TOWN OF BETHLEHEM" ❈

When the famous nineteenth-century preacher Phillips Brooks wrote his timeless poem that has become a beloved Christmas carol, he obviously was celebrating the fact for which Bethlehem is most famous. But the little town six miles from Jerusalem figures into other biblical stories.

Bethlehem was where Jacob and his family were headed when his wife, Rachel, died giving birth to Benjamin (Gen. 35:19). Rachel was subsequently buried just outside Bethlehem.

Ibzan, one of Israel's lesser-known judges, hailed from Bethlehem. The fact that he had thirty sons and thirty daughters was probably more noteworthy than the fact he was born in Bethlehem, spent his life there, and was buried there (Judg. 12:8).

Bethlehem was also home to that nameless Levite in Judges 17 who contracted with a man named Micah in the hill country of Ephraim to become his personal priest.

Bethlehem was the town from which Naomi and her family moved when they resettled in Moab. It was the town to which Naomi and her daughter-in-law returned following the deaths of her husband and her two sons (see Ruth). Bethlehem was where Ruth's celebrated great-grandson was born. Because King David was born in that little village, it became known as "the city of David."

Micah, an Old Testament prophet who lived seven hundred years before the birth of Christ, mentioned Bethlehem in his prophecy that the Messiah would be born there. "But you, Bethlehem Ephrathah, / though you are small among the clans of Judah, / out of you will come for me / one who will be ruler over Israel, / whose origins are from of old, / from ancient times" (Mic. 5:2).

❈ WOMEN YOU'D RATHER NOT BE MARRIED TO ❈

- Potiphar's wife: She unsuccessfully tried to seduce Joseph, then accused him of rape (Gen. 39:6–20).
- Jael, wife of Heber: She killed a man by using a hammer to drive a tent peg through his head while he was asleep in her tent (Judg. 4:17–21).
- Gomer, wife of Hosea: She was an adulterous woman (Hos. 1:2–3).
- Michal, wife of King David: She despised her husband, King David, for dancing and jumping before the Lord in worship (2 Sam. 6:14–16). And this, after David had gathered two hundred Philistine foreskins to make her his wife (1 Sam. 18:25–27.)
- Jezebel: The evil wife of Ahab slaughtered God's prophets (1 Kings 18:4).
- Witch of Endor: She practiced sorcery, which God condemned (Lev. 20:27; 1 Sam. 28:7–25). .
- Herodias: The wife of Herod requested that John the Baptist's head be cut off because he condemned her adultery (Matt. 14:3–12).

❈ THE MIRACLES OF THE APOSTLES ❈

In all likelihood, they couldn't believe their eyes—not only those who witnessed a supernatural healing or exorcism, but also those who were instruments of God's power. While some might think it was a miracle that the followers of Jesus actually got along and shared ("All the believers were one in heart and mind. No one claimed that any of his possessions was his own"—Acts 4:32), the apostles were the means of other more traditional miracles as well. Acts 5:12 says, "The apostles performed many miraculous signs and wonders among the people."

Peter is credited with the majority of them. By faith, Peter . . .

- walked on water alongside Jesus (Mark 6).
- healed a lame man at the Beautiful Gate (Acts 3).
- healed many as his shadow covered them (Acts 5).
- healed Aeneas (Acts 9).
- raised Dorcas from the dead (Acts 9).

❈ FASCINATING FACTS ABOUT ANGELS ❈

Angels are created by God (Gen. 2:1; Neh. 9:6; Eph. 3:9; Col. 1:16).

Angels are spirit beings (Ps. 104:4; Heb. 1:7, 14).

Angels are awesome creatures who inspire worship (Col. 2:18; Rev. 19:10; 22:9).

Angels report directly to God (Job 1:6; 2:1).

Angels were on the scene as God created the world (Job 38:5–7).

Angels announced Jesus's birth to the shepherds outside Bethlehem (Luke 2:10–14).

Angels don't marry (Matt. 22:30).

Angels exist forever (Rev. 4:8).

Angels exist to glorify God (Rev. 4:8).

Angels are sent to minister to and serve humans (Heb. 1:14).

Angels are innumerable (Ps. 68:17; Dan. 7:10).

Angels are intelligent beings (Dan. 9:21–22; 10:14).

Angels have a will (Isa. 14:12–15; Jude 6).

Angels express joy (Job 38:7; Luke 2:13).

Angels display desire (1 Pet. 1:12).

Angels are powerful and mighty (Ps. 103:20; 2 Thess. 1:7; 2 Pet. 2:11).

Angels fly (Dan. 9:21; Rev. 14:6).

Angels are not omnipresent, omnipotent, or omniscient
(Dan. 10:12–13; Jude 9; Matt. 24:36).

Angels are referred to a total of 273 times in thirty-four biblical books.

❈ THE TEN COMMANDMENTS ❈

1. You shall have no other gods before me.

2. You shall not make for yourself an idol in the form of anything in heaven above or on the earth beneath or in the waters below. You shall not bow down to them or worship them; for I, the LORD your God, am a jealous God, punishing the children for the sin of the fathers to the third and fourth generation of those who hate me, but showing love to a thousand generations of those who love me and keep my commandments.

3. You shall not misuse the name of the LORD your God, for the LORD will not hold anyone guiltless who misuses his name.

4. Remember the Sabbath day by keeping it holy. Six days you shall labor and do all your work, but the seventh day is a Sabbath to the LORD your God. On it you shall not do any work, neither you, nor your son or daughter, nor your manservant or maidservant, nor your animals, nor the alien within your gates. For in six days the LORD made the heavens and the earth, the sea, and all that is in them, but he rested on the seventh day. Therefore the LORD blessed the Sabbath day and made it holy.

5. Honor your father and your mother, so that you may live long in the land the LORD your God is giving you.

6. You shall not murder.

7. You shall not commit adultery.

8. You shall not steal.

9. You shall not give false testimony against your neighbor.

10. You shall not covet your neighbor's house. You shall not covet your neighbor's wife, or his manservant or maidservant, his ox or donkey, or anything that belongs to your neighbor.

(Exod. 20:1–17)

❈ DISEASES IN THE BIBLE ❈

- Barrenness (Gen. 16:1)
- Boils (Exod. 9:9; 2 Kings 20:7)
- The itch (Deut. 28:27)
- Lunacy (Deut. 28:28)
- Tumors (1 Sam. 5:6)
- Sunstroke or brain disorder (2 Kings 4:19)
- Leprosy (2 Kings 5:1)
- Fever (Matt. 8:14–15)
- Chronic hemorrhaging (Matt. 9:20)
- Blindness (Mark 10:46)
- Paralysis (Acts 8:7)

❋ PAGAN GODS OF THE BIBLE ❋

Name of God	Description	Reference
Asherah or (Ashtaroth)	Chief goddess of Tyre	Judges 6:25–28
Ashtoreths	Canaanite goddesses	1 Samuel 7:3–4
Baal	The chief deity of Canaan	1 Kings 18:17–40
Beelzebub	The prince of demons	Matthew 10:25; 12:24
Chemosh	The god of Moab	1 Kings 11:7
Dagon	Philistine agricultural god	1 Samuel 5:1–7; Judges 16:23–30
Diana (or Artemis)	Asiatic goddess with many breasts	Acts 19:27, 35
Jupiter (or Zeus)	The chief Roman god	Acts 14:12–13
Mercury (or Hermes)	Roman god of commerce	Acts 14:12
Merodach (or Marduk)	Chief god of Babylonians	Jeremiah 50:2
Molech	The god of the Ammonites	1 Kings 11:7
Nebo	Babylon's god of wisdom	Isaiah 46:1
Nishroch	An Assyrian god	2 Kings 19:37
Rimmon	A Syrian god	2 Kings 5:15–19
Tammuz	Goddess of fertility	Ezekiel 8:14
The unknown god	In Athens on Mars Hill	Acts 17:23

❋ MONEY, MONEY, MONEY, MONEY (MONEY) ❋

Currency	Value	Reference
Talent	60 minas (75 pounds or $1,000)	Matthew 25:15
Mina	60 shekels (600 grams)	Ezekiel 45:12
Shekel	2 bekas (2/5 ounce)	Exodus 30:13
Beka	10 gerahs (1/5 ounce)	Exodus 38:26
Gerah	1/50 ounce	Numbers 3:47
Kodrantes	A nickel	Matthew 5:26 (NIV note)
Denarius	A daily wage for a Roman	Matthew 20:2
A silver coin	40 denarii	Matthew 26:15
Assarion	A penny	Luke 12:6

❄ BIBLICAL CLAIMS OF THE DEITY OF JESUS ❄

- Jesus said, "I and the Father are one" (John 10:30).

- Jesus said, "Anyone who has seen me has seen the Father" (John 14:9).

- Jesus told the woman at the well he was the Messiah (John 4:25–26).

- Jesus affirmed Peter's statement that he was the Messiah and Son of God (Matt. 16:15–17; see also Mark 8:29–30; Luke 9:20–21).

- Jesus told the high priest that he was the Messiah and Son of God (Matt. 26:63–64; Mark 14:61–62).

- The Jews were aware that Jesus was making claims of being divine: "He was even calling God his own Father, making himself equal with God" (John 5:18).

- Jesus told the disciples, "You call me 'Teacher' and 'Lord,' and rightly so, for that is what I am" (John 13:13).

- Jesus claimed to forgive sins, which only God had the authority to do (Mark 2:5–11; Luke 5:20–24).

- Jesus admitted that he'd seen Abraham and even claimed to be eternal: "'I tell you the truth,' Jesus answered, 'before Abraham was born, I am!'" (John 8:57–58).

- Jesus said that he had seen God, which no one else could do (John 6:46).

- John wrote of Jesus, "In the beginning was the Word, and the Word was with God, and the Word was God. . . . And the Word became flesh and dwelt among us" (John 1:1, 14 RSV).

❄ APOSTOLIC FATHERS ❄

The Greek word translated "apostle" means "one who is sent out on a special assignment." The first Christians applied that definition to the disciples Jesus sent out to evangelize the world (Matt. 28:18–20). That list soon included Paul, whose dramatic conversion en route to persecute Christians in Damascus no one could contest. These individuals played a key role in planting churches in the first century.

Peter . . . . Spoke in Jerusalem on the Day of Pentecost and three thousand were saved. Many believe he was the head of the church in Jerusalem.

❈ APOSTOLIC FATHERS—CONT. ❈

Paul .... Wrote thirteen letters contained in the New Testament and made three mission trips to Roman provinces to evangelize the Gentiles.

John .... The disciple who claimed a uniquely close relationship with Jesus wrote a biography of the Savior's life embedded with many metaphors. Exiled on the island of Patmos from where he transcribed a vision he had of the risen Christ. We call that vision Revelation.

Matthew .... The converted tax collector wrote a biography of Jesus with a noticeable Jewish slant.

Thomas .... Legend suggests that he traveled to India to evangelize and plant a Christian church.

❈ JESUS'S PASSION FOR GOD THE FATHER ❈

- To those who sold doves he said, "Get these out of here! How dare you turn my Father's house into a market!" (John 2:16)

- "My food," said Jesus, "is to do the will of him who sent me and to finish his work." (John 4:34)

- For I have come down from heaven not to do my will but to do the will of him who sent me. (John 6:38)

- The one who sent me is with me; he has not left me alone, for I always do what pleases him. (John 8:29)

- The world must learn that I love the Father and that I do exactly what my Father has commanded me. (John 14:31)

- If you obey my commands, you will remain in my love, just as I have obeyed my Father's commands and remain in his love. (John 15:10)

✻ GREAT ESCAPES ✺

Drama and suspense punctuate the pages of the Bible. No wonder so many Hollywood scriptwriters have based films on biblical stories and characters. One of the recurring dramatic themes of Scripture is that of people who escaped a threatening situation by the skin of their teeth or in a seemingly miraculous way.

- **Lot** escaped the destruction of Sodom and Gomorrah. When God judged the twin cities, he sent two angels to lead Abraham's nephew and family away before the annihilation began (Gen. 19).

- **Joseph's brothers** ditched him and were about to leave him for dead when they saw an approaching caravan bound for Egypt. They decided to sell their brother instead of just letting him die of thirst, so Joseph escaped certain death and went on to become Pharaoh's right-hand regent (Gen. 37, 39–41).

- **Moses** escaped a death sentence through the disobedience of his mother. When Pharaoh saw that the population of the Israelites in Egypt was increasing, he ordered that baby boys born to Hebrew women be slaughtered. Moses's mother hid her son in a basket in the Nile River. When the baby was discovered and taken to Pharaoh's daughter, she adopted him. Because his life was spared, he grew up to become the one who led the Israelites out of Egypt (Exod. 1–2).

- **The Israelites** escaped the Egyptian army that pursued them when God miraculously divided the Red Sea, allowing them to cross. Just as the army reached the dry bed of the sea, God drowned them as the waters found their natural level (Exod. 14).

- **God called Jonah** to go preach to the pagan city of Nineveh. He resisted, ran in the opposite direction, and boarded a ship. When the ship began to sink in a storm, Jonah recognized that his disobedience was a likely cause. The sailors threw the rebellious prophet overboard. But God arranged for a big fish to swallow him, and he lived in the fish's belly for three days before being spit up on shore (Jon. 1).

- **Mary, Joseph, and the baby Jesus** narrowly escaped the bloody massacre of male babies in Bethlehem that King Herod ordered. Being warned in a dream to run for their lives, the holy family traveled to Egypt (Matt. 2).

- **King Herod imprisoned Peter** in an attempt to persecute Christ's followers and please the Jews. The night before Peter's trial was to begin, an angel supernaturally sprang him from his cell in spite of the fact he was chained to two soldiers (Acts 12).

■ **Paul** was the object of a death threat when Jews in Damascus learned of his conversion. When the Christians in the city discovered the plot, they lowered Paul in a woven basket over the city wall under the cover of darkness (Acts 9).

❈ SIGNIFICANT TREES ❈

Kind of Tree	Significance	Reference
Tree of the knowledge of good and evil	Adam and Eve were warned not to eat from its fruit.	Genesis 2:17
Tree of life	Adam and Eve were kept from this tree so they wouldn't live forever in their sinful state.	Genesis 3:24
Great trees of Mamre	Abraham pitched his tents in this grove while living in Hebron.	Genesis 13:18
Large oak tree in the forest of Ephraim	Absalom's long hair got tangled in the branches, which resulted in his death.	2 Samuel 18:9
Singing trees	A metaphor of creation's desire to praise the Lord.	Psalm 96:12
Mount of Olives	A grove of olive trees overlooking Jerusalem where Jesus often prayed.	Mark 13:3
Jericho's sycamore-fig tree	What Zacchaeus climbed to see Jesus.	Luke 19:4
Jesus's cross	Peter refers to the cross on which Jesus died as "the tree."	1 Peter 2:24
Tree of life	Perhaps the same tree from the Garden of Eden now planted and growing in the New Jerusalem.	Revelation 22:2

❊ STARS AND CONSTELLATIONS ❊
MENTIONED IN THE BIBLE

From the very beginning of the Bible, its writers frequently mentioned stars. In the account of creation found in Genesis, the writer described how God caused them to come into existence as part of the created order. "He made the stars also" (Gen. 1:16 RSV). Psalm 8 documents how David felt dwarfed by the countless stars in the sky as he gazed upward.

> When I consider your heavens,
>   the work of your fingers,
> the moon and the stars,
>   which you have set in place,
> what is man that you are mindful of him,
>   the son of man that you care for him? (Ps. 8:3–4)

Although the Scriptures offer no indication that mankind should seek guidance from the stars, the stars do offer a sense of direction. Numerous verses suggest the stars point to the Creator and motivate those who bear the Creator's image to worship him. Perhaps that is why Jesus, the ultimate God-pointer, is referred to as "the bright and morning star" (Rev. 22:16 KJV).

In Matthew the Magi from the east were guided in some sense by a star. Many think this unusual light in the night sky was an alignment of planets. Perhaps God used such an astronomical sign as a way to get the attention of pagan stargazers who attempted to find truth in the heavens. We do know that the constellations we recognize were clear to those in the Old Testament. The book of Job makes reference to some of them:

- He is the Maker of the Bear and Orion, / the Pleiades and the constellations of the south. (Job 9:9)
- Can you bind the beautiful Pleiades? / Can you loose the cords of Orion? / Can you bring forth the constellations in their seasons / or lead out the Bear with its cubs? (Job 38:31–33)

❊ FAMOUS PAIRS ❊

Adam and Eve (Gen. 2) • Abraham and Sarah (Gen. 12–17) •
Ruth and Boaz (Ruth 2) • David and Jonathan (1 Sam. 20) • David and
Bathsheba (2 Sam. 11) • Mary and Martha (Luke 10) • Ananias and Sapphira
(Acts 5) • Paul and Silas (Acts 16) • Priscilla and Aquila (Acts 18)

❄ BUILDING MATERIALS MENTIONED IN THE BIBLE ❄

Material	Used for	Reference
Gopher wood	Noah's ark	Genesis 6 (KJV)
Acacia wood	Ark of the covenant	Exodus 25
Cedar planks	Solomon's temple	1 Kings 5
Pine logs	Solomon's temple	1 Kings 5
Olive wood	Solomon's temple	1 Kings 6
Hewn stone	Solomon's temple	1 Kings 6 (RSV)
Dressed stone	Solomon's temple	1 Kings 6
Silver	Statue	Daniel 2
Iron	Statue	Daniel 2
Clay roof	House rooftop	Mark 2 (NLT)
Costly stones, wood, hay, and stubble	Building on the foundation of faith in Christ	1 Corinthians 3 ("stubble"—KJV)
Gold	Streets of the New Jerusalem	Revelation 21

❄ THE FOUR HORSEMEN ❄

Revelation 6:1–8 describes the four horsemen of the Apocalypse. They are symbolic descriptions of what will take place in the end times.

The first horseman is mentioned in Revelation 6:2. He quite possibly refers to the Antichrist, who will be given authority and will conquer all who oppose him. Curiously, the Antichrist, who is the false imitator of the true Christ, rides the same color horse that Jesus is symbolically pictured on at his return (Rev. 19:11–16).

The second horseman is mentioned in Revelation 6:4. He refers to terrible warfare that will break out in the end times.

The third horseman is described in Revelation 6:5–6. He refers to a great famine that will take place, which may be the result of the wars from the second horseman. Food will be in short supply, while such things as wine and oil will not be.

The fourth horseman is mentioned in Revelation 6:8. He is symbolic of death and devastation and follows quite logically from the horsemen that precede him. The fourth will bring further warfare and terrible famines, along with awful plagues and diseases.

❀ THINGS GOD HATES ❀

A proud look (Prov. 6:17 NKJV) • A lying tongue (Prov. 6:17 NKJV) •
Hands that shed innocent blood (Prov. 6:17 NKJV) • A heart that devises
wicked plans (Prov. 6:18 NKJV) • Feet that are swift in running to evil (Prov. 6:18
NKJV) • A false witness who speaks lies (Prov. 6:19 NKJV) • One who sows
discord among brethren (Prov. 6:19 NKJV) • Divorce (Mal. 2:16 NKJV)

❀ CRITICS AND NAYSAYERS ❀

From the opening pages of Genesis we find those who take exception with God's
direction. But there are also those who are critical of the people who walk away
from what God wants. Here are a few examples of both:

- **The serpent** in the Garden of Eden questioned God's prohibition of eating from the tree of the knowledge of good and evil (Gen. 3).

- **Pharaoh** was critical of Moses's request to "let my people go" (Exod. 5).

- **Joseph's brothers** mocked him when he made reference to his dreams (Gen. 37).

- **Goliath** mocked Israel and thus Israel's God (1 Sam. 17).

- **Nathan** the prophet was critical of David when Israel's king failed to acknowledge his sin with Bathsheba (2 Sam. 12).

- **Job's three friends** questioned his integrity when the innocent victim found himself the epitome of human suffering (Job 2).

- **Shimei**, a relative of King Saul, bad-mouthed David as he fled from Absalom's attempts to overthrow him (2 Sam. 16).

- **Elijah** criticized the prophets of Baal when their attempts to prove Baal's existence failed (1 Kings 18).

- **Haman** was critical of Esther's relative Mordecai, but his hatred extended to all those of Jewish extraction (Esther 3).

- **Peter** denounced Jesus for making statements that indicated he would suffer and die as part of his earthly mission (Matt. 16).

- **Judas Iscariot** criticized the woman who poured expensive perfume over Jesus's feet, claiming it should have been sold to give the proceeds to the poor (Mark 14).

- **The Pharisees and chief priests** were highly critical of Jesus's interpretation of the Law (Mark 2–3).

❧ GENEALOGY FOOTNOTES ❧

Genealogies may be the most underappreciated pages in the Bible. Except for their use as a nonmedicinal remedy for insomnia, they fail to capture the attention of the average reader. A careful look, however, at these lists of unpronounceable names will yield curious findings. A case in point is the genealogy found in 1 Chronicles. One name is listed after another ad infinitum until chapter 4, verses 9–10: "Jabez was more honorable than his brothers. His mother had named him Jabez, saying, 'I gave birth to him in pain.' Jabez cried out to the God of Israel, 'Oh, that you would bless me and enlarge my territory! Let your hand be with me, and keep me from harm so that I will be free from pain.' And God granted his request."

In Matthew we find an ancestral log of the ancestors of Jesus. There is another one in Luke. A careful comparison reveals that Matthew traces Jesus's formal genealogy through Joseph back to Abraham (the symbol of those who believed God), whereas Luke apparently traces his origins through his earthly mother to Adam (demonstrating his relationship to the entire human family).

❧ THE KINGS OF ISRAEL AND THEIR FATES ❧

Here is a list of some of the most famous (or most interesting) Israel's kings and their fates:

King	*Description*	*Reference*
Saul	Rejected by God; committed suicide by falling on his sword	1 Samuel 13; 31
David	Blessed by God (although imperfect) and curried favor with his subjects	2 Samuel 5
Solomon	Allowed by God to excel in wisdom and to build the temple, but Solomon embraced the pagan ways of his seven hundred wives	1 Kings 11
Jeroboam (Israel)	Perverted the worship of God	1 Kings 12
Rehoboam (Judah)	Started a civil war with Israel due to his stupidity	1 Kings 14
Amon	Assassinated by his officials	2 Kings 21
Zedekiah	Had his eyes plucked out, was bound in shackles, and was taken into captivity	2 Kings 25

❀ LIFE BEHIND BARS ❀

The biblical writers make reference to those in prison in two different ways. On the one hand, they mention those who are imprisoned unjustly; on the other hand, they point to those who are jailed for just causes but who are the object of God's mercy.

Biblical Prisoners	*Reference*
Joseph	Genesis 39
Shadrach, Meshach, and Abednego	Daniel 3
Daniel	Daniel 6
Jeremiah	Jeremiah 20
John the Baptist	Mark 6
Barabbas	Mark 15
Peter and John	Acts 4
Paul and Silas	Acts 16
John	Revelation 1
Satan	Revelation 20

God's Concern for Prisoners	*Reference*
To proclaim freedom for the captives and release from darkness for the prisoners	Isaiah 61; Luke 4
"I was in prison and you came to visit me"	Matthew 25
Others were chained and put in prison	Hebrews 11
He leads forth the prisoners with singing	Psalm 68

❀ NAMES FOR JESUS ❀

Alpha and Omega (Rev. 1:8) • Author and Perfecter of faith (Heb. 12:2) • Bright Morning Star (Rev. 22:16) • Carpenter's Son (Matt. 13:55) • Chief Shepherd (1 Pet. 5:4) • Christ (Matt. 1:16) • Consolation of Israel (Luke 2:25) • Dayspring from on high (Luke 1:78 KJV) • Immanuel (Matt. 1:23) • Friend of Sinners (Matt. 11:19) • Good Shepherd (John 10:11) • Great Shepherd (Heb. 13:20) • Lamb of God (John 1:29) • Light of the World (John 9:5) • Lion of Judah (Rev. 5:5) • Messiah (John 1:41) • Rabbi (John 3:2) • Last Adam (1 Cor. 15:45) • Son of David (Matt. 15:22) • Son of God (Luke 1:35) • Son of Man (Matt. 20:18)

❋ CITIES OF REFUGE ❋

A just and merciful God determined that when the Israelites took possession of the Land of Promise, they should establish cities of refuge. These were places of safety for someone who had accidentally killed another person. He could go to the city to escape the vengeance of relatives or friends and there await a trial to officially determine his guilt or innocence. These cities were not places to escape justice, but rather places where justice would be carried out.

> So they set apart **Kedesh** in Galilee in the hill country of Naphtali, **Shechem** in the hill country of Ephraim, and Kiriath Arba (that is, **Hebron**), in the hill country of Judah. On the east side of the Jordan of Jericho they designated **Bezer** in the desert on the plateau in the tribe of Reuben, **Ramoth** in Gilead in the tribe of Gad, and **Golan** in Bashan in the tribe of Manasseh. Any of the Israelites or any alien living among them who killed someone accidentally could flee to these designated cities and not be killed by the avenger of blood prior to standing trial before the assembly. (Josh. 20:7–9)

❋ WHAT THE BIBLE SAYS ABOUT THE BIBLE ❋

- Above all, you must understand that no prophecy of Scripture came about by the prophet's own interpretation. For prophecy never had its origin in the will of man, but men spoke from God as they were carried along by the Holy Spirit. (2 Pet. 1:20–21)
- For the word of God is living and active. Sharper than any double-edged sword, it penetrates even to dividing soul and spirit, joints and marrow; it judges the thoughts and attitudes of the heart. (Heb. 4:12)
- All Scripture is God-breathed and is useful for teaching, rebuking, correcting and training in righteousness, so that the man of God may be thoroughly equipped for every good work. (2 Tim. 3:16–17)
- "Is not my word like fire," declares the LORD, "and like a hammer that breaks a rock in pieces?" (Jer. 23:29)
- Do not let this Book of the Law depart from your mouth; meditate on it day and night, so that you may be careful to do everything written in it. Then you will be prosperous and successful. (Josh. 1:8)
- The grass withers and the flowers fall, / but the word of our God stands forever. (Isa. 40:8)
- Heaven and earth will pass away, but my words will never pass away. (Mark 13:31)

❈ QUESTIONS FROM THE CREATOR ❈

Question Asked	To Whom	Reference
Where are you?	Adam	Genesis 3:9
Where is your brother?	Cain	Genesis 4:9
What is that in your hand?	Moses	Exodus 4:2
What about your brother, Aaron the Levite?	Moses	Exodus 4:14
Have you considered my servant Job?	Satan	Job 1:8
Where were you when I laid the earth's foundation?	Job	Job 38:4
To whom will you compare me?	Israel	Isaiah 40:25
Can a mother forget the baby at her breast?	Israel	Isaiah 49:15
When men fall down, do they not get up?	Israel	Jeremiah 8:4
If you have raced with men on foot / and they have worn you out, / how can you compete with horses?	Israel	Jeremiah 12:5
Can a man bear children?	Israel	Jeremiah 30:6
Son of man, can these bones live?	Ezekiel	Ezekiel 37:3
Should I not be concerned about that great city?	Jonah	Jonah 4:11
And what does the LORD require of you?	Israel	Micah 6:8
Will a man rob God?	Israel	Malachi 3:8

❈ BIBLICAL CHARACTERS FROM AFRICA ❈

- In Genesis 41 we read of Joseph's two sons (Ephraim and Manasseh), whose mother was an Egyptian.
- In Numbers 12 we read of Moses's marrying a Cushite wife (Cush was in the southern Nile Valley of North Africa).
- In 1 Kings 9 we read that Solomon married a daughter of the Egyptian pharaoh.
- In 1 Kings 10 we read of the queen of Sheba, who came to visit King Solomon.
- In Jeremiah 13 the color of the Ethiopians' skin is referred to as unchangeable.
- In Luke 23 we read of Simon of Cyrene, who was forced to carry Jesus's cross.
- In Acts 8 we read of Candace, who was the queen of the Ethiopians.
- In Acts 8 we read of an Ethiopian eunuch who was in charge of the treasury of Ethiopia's queen.

❀ WHAT WILL HEAVEN BE LIKE? ❀

There will be no
- tears (Rev. 7:17).
- sickness (Rev. 22:2).
- pain (Rev. 21:4).
- death (1 Cor. 15:26; Rev. 21:4).
- hunger or thirst (Rev. 7:16).
- sin (Rev. 21:27).
- night (Rev. 21:25).
- need for sun or moon (Rev. 21:23).

The heavenly city
- is shaped like a cube with its width, length, and height being equal (Rev. 21:16).
- is approximately fourteen hundred miles long, wide, and high (Rev. 21:16).
- is built upon a foundation of twelve layers of stones. Each layer is inlaid with a different precious gem (Rev. 21:19–20).

The wall around the city
- is made of pure jasper and is about two hundred feet high (Rev. 21:17–18).
- has twelve gates (Rev. 21:12).

The main street
- will be made of transparent gold (Rev. 21:21).

God
- will rule from his throne, which will be in the very center (Rev. 4:2–6; 22:1).
- will dwell with man forever (Rev. 21:3).

❀ NEW TESTAMENT CHURCHES ❀

Antioch of Pisidia . . . . Acts 13:14	Laodicea . . . . Revelation 3:14–22
Antioch of Syria . . . . Acts 11:19	Lystra . . . . Acts 14:6
Athens . . . . Acts 17:34	Pergamum . . . . Revelation 2:12–17
"Babylon" . . . . 1 Peter 5:13	Philadelphia Revelation 3:7–13
Berea . . . . Acts 17:11	Philippi . . . . Acts 16:15, 40;
Colosse . . . . Colossians 1:2, 27	Philippians 1:1
Corinth . . . . Acts 18:1	Rome . . . . Romans 1:7
Derbe . . . . Acts 14:20–22	Sardis . . . . Revelation 3:1–6
Ephesus . . . . Acts 18:19	Smyrna . . . . Revelation 2:8–11
Galatia . . . . Galatians 1:2, 6–9	Thessalonica . . . . Acts 17:1
Iconium . . . . Acts 14:2	Thyatira . . . . Revelation 2:18–29
Jerusalem . . . . Acts 2:41–47	Troas . . . . Acts 20:7–12

❈ THE GOSPEL IN ONE VERSE ❈

The most famous of all verses in the entire New Testament is John 3:16. "For God so loved the world that he gave his one and only Son, that whoever believes in him shall not perish but have eternal life." The essence of the Christian gospel is contained in these familiar words Jesus originally spoke.

God so loved the world: The One who created the universe and mankind is a holy God who must judge sin in order to maintain the integrity of his holiness. But he loves those he created in his image.

He gave his one and only Son: The proof of God's love is apparent in his willingness to give Jesus (the physical expression of his spiritual essence) as a sacrifice for the sin of the world to fulfill the demands his holiness dictates.

Whosoever believes: Although God's overture of love is mind-boggling, it is not automatic. Those who are willing to admit their guilt and acknowledge their need of a Savior must personally appropriate the death of God's sinless Son on a Roman cross. The atoning death of God's sinless Son on a Roman cross is applied only to those who possess a genuine faith in Jesus.

Shall not perish: Even though sinful people (by definition) are separated from a holy God, the Creator will not judge or condemn those who accept Jesus's death as their substitute and claim the forgiveness God offers them.

But have eternal life: Christ's transaction on the cross is a lifetime warranty that entitles those who have "believed" to enjoy the presence of God in this life and beyond the borders of death.

❈ FAMOUS ANGELS OF THE BIBLE ❈

Angels in the Bible didn't sign autographs, but they did have the aura of celebrities. Most of the heavenly beings didn't have wings, harps, or names, though cherubim (Gen. 3) and seraphim (Isa. 6) had wings. The word translated "angel" in the New Testament simply meant "messenger." The assumption is that they were non-human beings on assignment with a message to someone or some group of people. The two archangels named in Scripture are Michael and Gabriel. Michael is credited with protecting Israel (Dan. 10), whereas Gabriel interpreted Daniel's visions (Dan. 9). He is also the one who informed both Zechariah and Mary of unexpected pregnancies (Luke 1) that changed the course of history.

❄ FORBIDDEN FOODS ❄

According to Leviticus 11 and Deuteronomy 14, not all foods were created equal. God informed Moses that certain animals were "clean" and some were "unclean," and he commanded his people to avoid eating the latter. Here's how to tell the difference.

Clean and edible:
All animals were considered acceptable that had cloven hoofs and chewed the cud, including cattle, goats, sheep, and deer. All fish with fins and scales, and insects of the locust family, were on the "okay to eat" list.

Unclean and inedible delicacies:
The pig and the camel were off-limits. So also were carnivorous birds, sea creatures without fins and scales, most insects (darn!), rodents, and reptiles.

Cooking precautions:
Sometimes biblical writers also added warning labels to keep the people of God on their restrictive diet. For example, in Exodus 23:19 we read, "Do not cook a young goat in its mother's milk."

❄ WHAT'S IN A NAME? ❄

Name	*Meaning*
Adam	Man or mankind
Abram	Exalted father
Abraham	Father of a multitude
Sarai/Sarah	Princess
Ishmael	God hears
Isaac	He laughs
Jacob	He cheats, or he grasps the heel
Reuben	See, a son
Joseph	May he add
Israel	He strives with God, or God strives
Benjamin	Son of my right hand
Naomi	Pleasant
Malachi	My messenger
Barnabas	Son of encouragement

❄ DREAMS ❄

Sometimes portions of the Bible appear to be the perfect remedy for insomnia. Reading through the names of the various genealogies might have the same effect as counting sheep. But then again, some of the more interesting stories in the Scriptures pertain to those who were asleep. Dreams figure prominently in both the Old and New Testaments.

Name of Dreamer	Setting	Reference
Jacob	Dreamed God confirmed that he would fulfill what he promised Abraham	Genesis 28
Joseph	Dreamed his brothers would worship him	Genesis 37
Cupbearer to Pharaoh	Dreamed he'd be restored	Genesis 40
Pharaoh's baker	Dreamed he'd be beheaded	Genesis 40
Pharaoh	Dreamed of coming famine	Genesis 41
Solomon	Dreamed that God gave him wisdom and a warning	1 Kings 3; 9
Joseph of Nazareth	Dreamed that an angel told him Mary was pure and he could marry her	Matthew 1
Joseph of Nazareth	Dreamed about the need to flee from Bethlehem to Egypt to escape danger	Matthew 2
Joseph of Nazareth	Dreamed that it was safe to return to Israel because Herod the Great was dead	Matthew 2
Magi from the East	Dreamed it was unsafe to return to their homeland the same way they came	Matthew 2

❄ THE SKINNY ON GOLIATH ❄

Goliath was from Gath. • He fought for the Philistine army. •
He was over nine feet tall. • He wore a bronze helmet. • His armor weighed
125 pounds. • The iron point on his spear weighed fifteen pounds. •
He had four brothers. • Once Goliath was beheaded with his own weapon,
his sword was kept by the priest in Nob, wrapped in a cloth as a relic.

- For from him and through him / and to him are all things. / To him be the glory forever! / Amen. (Rom. 11:36)

- For my own sake, for my own sake, / I do it, / for how should my name be profaned? / My glory I will not give to another. (Isa. 48:11 ESV)

- Then all your people *will be* righteous; / They will possess the land forever, / The branch of My planting, / The work of My hands, / That I may be glorified. (Isa. 60:21 NASB)

- In bringing many sons to glory, it was fitting that God, for whom and through whom everything exists, should make the author of their salvation perfect through suffering. (Heb. 2:10)

- For by Him all things were created, both in the heavens and on earth, visible and invisible, whether thrones or dominions or rulers or authorities—all things have been created through Him and for Him. (Col. 1:16 NASB)

- The LORD hath made all things for himself: yea, even the wicked for the day of evil. (Prov. 16:4 KJV)

- I will say to the north, "Give them up!" / and to the south, "Do not hold them back." / Bring my sons from afar / and my daughters from the ends of the earth— / everyone who is called by my name, / whom I created for my glory, / whom I formed and made. (Isa. 43:6–7)

- For as the waistcloth clings to the loins of a man, so I made the whole house of Israel and the whole house of Judah cling to me, says the LORD, that they might be for me a people, a name, a praise, and a glory, but they would not listen. (Jer. 13:11 RSV)

- He predestined us to be adopted as his sons through Jesus Christ, in accordance with his pleasure and will—to the praise of his glorious grace. (Eph. 1:5–6)

- When he comes to be glorified by his saints and to be marveled at on that day among all who have believed, because our testimony to you was believed. (2 Thess. 1:10 NRSV)

❈ THE ATTRIBUTES OF GOD ❈

Omnipresent • Supreme • Sovereign • Immutable • Omniscient • Holy • Omnipotent • Faithful • Good • Patient • Gracious • Merciful • Loving • Wrathful

❀ KING DAVID'S DYSFUNCTIONAL FAMILY ❀

Name	Issue	Reference
David's wife, Michal	Had a fit over her husband dancing before the Lord in a loincloth.	2 Samuel 6
Bathsheba	David seduced her, got her pregnant, and then married her after having her husband, Uriah, murdered.	2 Samuel 11
Amnon	Feigned sickness so his half sister Tamar would attend to his needs, then he raped her.	2 Samuel 13
Absalom	Had his brother Amnon murdered for what he had done to his sister and then became a fugitive in Geshur. Absalom also attempted to usurp the throne of his father, King David.	2 Samuel 13–18
David	Even though David grieved for Absalom while he was on the run, once he returned to Jerusalem, the king refused to see him.	2 Samuel 14
Adonijah	Without David's knowing it, this egotistical son ascended his father's throne and claimed the crown.	1 Kings 1
Solomon	In spite of praying for wisdom instead of great riches, the son of David who became king foolishly married seven hundred wives and slept with three hundred concubines.	1 Kings 11

❀ SONGS OF ASCENT ❀

The Songs of Ascent refer to Psalms 120–134. The children of Israel reportedly sang these songs as they made annual pilgrimages to Jerusalem. Since the ancient city of Jerusalem (and its temple) was elevated above sea level, pilgrims making their way to the religious festivals ascended as they drew near on foot. One of the first psalms in this collection of hill-climbing choruses appropriately begins, "I lift up my eyes to the hills— / where does my help come from?" (Ps. 121:1).

❧ THE TOP 50 MOST MEMORIZED ❧
PASSAGES OF THE BIBLE

1. Genesis 1:1
2. Psalm 1
3. Psalm 23
4. Psalm 27:4
5. Psalm 46:1
6. Psalm 46:10
7. Psalm 119:11
8. Proverbs 3:5–6
9. Proverbs 22:6
10. Ecclesiastes 3:1–8
11. Isaiah 40:31
12. Isaiah 53
13. Matthew 4:4
14. Matthew 5:3–12
15. Matthew 6:9–13
16. Matthew 7:12
17. Matthew 11:28–30
18. Matthew 28:19–20
19. Luke 9:23
20. John 1:12
21. John 1:14
22. John 3:16
23. John 4:23
24. John 14:2–3
25. John 14:26
26. Acts 1:8
27. Acts 20:35
28. Romans 1:16
29. Romans 3:23
30. Romans 5:8
31. Romans 6:23
32. Romans 8:37
33. Romans 12:1
34. 1 Corinthians 10:13
35. 2 Corinthians 12:9
36. Galatians 2:20
37. Galatians 6:7
38. Ephesians 2:8–9
39. Philippians 2:3–4
40. Philippians 4:6–7
41. Philippians 4:13
42. Philippians 4:19
43. Colossians 2:6–7
44. 1 Thessalonians 4:15–17
45. Hebrews 4:12
46. Hebrews 4:15–16
47. Hebrews 11:6
48. James 1:5
49. James 1:19–20
50. Revelation 3:20

❧ GARDENS OF THE BIBLE ❧

Name of Garden	What Happened There	Reference
Garden of God	Where Lucifer lived before he was thrown out of heaven	Ezekiel 28:11–17
Garden of Eden	Where Adam and Eve enjoyed paradise until they gave in to the serpent's temptation	Genesis 2:8–3:24
Garden of Gethsemane	Where Jesus prayed the night before he was crucified; the place where Judas betrayed him with a kiss	Matthew 26:36
Garden of Resurrection	Where Jesus was buried after the Crucifixion and where the women came to anoint his body with spices, only to discover his tomb was empty	John 19:41–20:18

❧ VERSES RELATING HAPPINESS ❧
WITH KNOWING GOD

- It was Jesus who said, "The thief comes only to steal and kill and destroy; I have come that they may have life, and have it to the full" (John 10:10).
- Telling the parable of talents, Jesus referred to himself as the master who invited his obedient servants to "come and share your master's happiness" (Matt. 25:21).
- Jesus declares that whoever comes to him will be spiritually filled: "I am the bread of life. He who comes to me will never go hungry, and he who believes in me will never be thirsty" (John 6:35).
- In Ecclesiastes 2:26 we see that God himself gives happiness: "To the man who pleases him, God gives wisdom, knowledge and happiness."
- The Sermon on the Mount begins with Jesus saying, "Blessed are the . . ." In essence, however, the word *blessed* could be replaced with the word *happy*. Jesus begins the most famous of all sermons postulating that true happiness comes to those who are "poor in spirit," those who "mourn," the "meek," those who "hunger and thirst for righteousness," the "merciful," the "pure in heart," the "peacemakers," and the "persecuted" (Matt. 5:3–10).
- When Jesus told the parable of the lost sheep, he likened himself to the shepherd who went searching: "And if he finds it, I tell you the truth, he is happier about that one sheep than about the ninety-nine that did not wander off" (Matt. 18:13).
- As Jesus gave his disciples reasons to be trusting of the Father's daily provision, he told them God actually finds joy in caring for them. "Do not be afraid, little flock, for your Father has chosen gladly to give you the kingdom" (Luke 12:32 NASB).
- Jesus declares that he desires his happiness to be in his people. "I have told you this so that my joy may be in you and that your joy may be complete" (John 15:11).

❧ SOLOMON'S THRONE ❧

Solomon built himself a uniquely impressive throne. The Bible gives this brief description:

> Then the king made a great throne inlaid with ivory and overlaid with fine gold. The throne had six steps, and its back had a rounded top. On both sides of the seat were armrests, with a lion standing beside each of them. Twelve lions stood on the six steps, one at either end of each step. Nothing like it had ever been made for any other kingdom. (1 Kings 10:18–20)

❧ QUOTES YOU WON'T FIND IN THE BIBLE, ❧ NO MATTER HOW HARD YOU LOOK

- Early to bed, early to rise, makes a man healthy, wealthy, and wise.
- A penny saved is a penny earned.
- God helps those who help themselves.
- All's fair in love and war.
- All's well that ends well.
- Only the good die young.
- A shared joy is a doubled joy. A shared sorrow is half a sorrow.
- Money is the root of all evil.
- Beauty is only skin-deep.
- Cleanliness is next to godliness.
- Laughter is the best medicine.
- Actions speak louder than words.
- United we stand, divided we fall.
- Love means never having to say you're sorry.
- You can't judge a book by its cover.
- Don't judge another until you've walked a mile in his shoes.
- Grief often treads upon the heels of pleasure.
- Sin is not hurtful because it is forbidden; it is forbidden because it is hurtful.
- Don't put all your eggs in one basket.
- Experience is the best teacher.
- Good fences make good neighbors.

❧ PUT ON YOUR DANCING SHOES ❧

According to biblical reference, dancing is an appropriate response when the circumstances of life awaken joy in the human heart. King Solomon declared that different seasons call for different responses, "a time to mourn and a time to dance" (Eccl. 3:4). The psalmist even indicated that the Lord prompts dancing: "You turned my wailing into dancing" (Ps. 30:11).

But the Bible also identifies dancing as a vehicle for communicating praise to God. In Psalm 149:3 the writer instructed: "Let them praise his name with dancing." Perhaps the most graphic portrait of kicking up one's heels in unrestrained joy and worship is the picture in 2 Samuel 6, where Israel's king was overcome with emotion as the ark of the covenant was returned to Jerusalem after a lengthy time in exile. David shed his regal robes and danced before the Lord.

THE "HARD" SAYINGS OF JESUS

- I tell you the truth, unless you eat the flesh of the Son of Man and drink his blood, you have no life in you. Whoever eats my flesh and drinks my blood has eternal life, and I will raise him up at the last day. (John 6:53)
- I tell you the truth, it is hard for a rich man to enter the kingdom of heaven. Again I tell you, it is easier for a camel to go through the eye of a needle than for a rich man to enter the kingdom of God. (Matt. 19:23)
- If anyone comes to me and does not hate his father and mother, his wife and children, his brothers and sisters—yes, even his own life—he cannot be my disciple. (Luke 14:26)
- Let the dead bury their own dead, but you go and proclaim the kingdom of God. (Luke 9:60)
- My God, my God, why have you forsaken me? (Matt. 27:46)
- Moses permitted you to divorce your wives because your hearts were hard. But it was not that way from the beginning. I tell you that anyone who divorces his wife, except for marital unfaithfulness, and marries another woman commits adultery. (Matt. 19:8–9)
- Do not suppose that I have come to bring peace on earth. I did not come to bring peace, but a sword. For I have come to turn / "a man against his father, / a daughter against her mother, / a daughter-in-law against her mother-in-law— / a man's enemies will be the members of his own household." / Anyone who loves his father or mother more than me is not worthy of me. (Matt. 10:34–37)

THE TEN SHORTEST BOOKS IN THE BIBLE

Book	*Length*
2 John	13 verses
3 John	14 verses
Obadiah	21 verses
Philemon	25 verses
Jude	25 verses
Haggai	38 verses
Nahum	47 verses
Jonah	48 verses
Habakkuk	56 verses
Joel	73 verses

❧ QUEENS OF THE BIBLE ❧

Name	Nationality	References
Michal	Israelite	2 Samuel 6:20–23
Bathsheba	Israelite	2 Samuel 11–12
The Queen of Sheba	Sheban	1 Kings 10; 2 Chronicles 9; Matthew 12:42; Luke 11:31
Maacah	Israelite	1 Kings 15:10–13; 2 Chronicles 15:16
Jezebel	Sidonian	1 Kings 16:31
Athaliah	Israelite	2 Kings 11
Nehushta	Israelite	2 Kings 24:8–16
The Queen of Babylon	Babylonian	Daniel 5:10–12
Vashti	Persian	Esther 1
Esther	Jewish	Esther 2–10
Herodias	Jewish	Matthew 14:1–12
Candace	Ethiopian	Acts 8:27

❧ DEVIOUS PLOTS ❧

- Cain plotted to kill Abel (Gen. 4).
- Jacob plotted to steal his brother's birthright (Gen. 27).
- Joseph's brothers plotted to sell him into slavery and feign his death (Gen. 37).
- Haman plotted to have all the Jews exterminated (Esther 3).
- David plotted to have Uriah murdered so he could legally marry Bathsheba (2 Sam. 11).
- Jezebel plotted to murder Elijah (1 Kings 19).
- Sanballat plotted to undermine Nehemiah's wall-building project (Neh. 4).
- The satraps plotted against Daniel and had him thrown to the lions (Dan. 6).
- Herod plotted to have the male infants in Bethlehem murdered (Matt. 2).
- Herodius plotted to have John the Baptist beheaded (Mark 6).
- Judas Iscariot plotted to have Jesus arrested by the chief priests (Luke 22).
- Ananias and Sapphira plotted to deceive the leaders of the Jerusalem church (Acts 5).
- Simon Magnus plotted to find a way to purchase the power associated with the Holy Spirit (Acts 8).

❧ SIGNS THAT THE END OF THE ❧ WORLD MAY BE NEAR

- Many will come claiming to be Christ and will deceive many (Matt. 24:5).
- There will be wars and rumors of wars (Matt. 24:6).
- Famines and earthquakes will occur in various places (Matt. 24:7).
- "People will be lovers of themselves, lovers of money, boastful, proud, abusive, disobedient to their parents, ungrateful, unholy, without love, unforgiving, slanderous, without self-control, brutal, not lovers of the good, treacherous, rash, conceited, lovers of pleasure rather than lovers of God—having a form of godliness but denying its power" (2 Tim. 3:2–5).
- God says that in the last days: "I will pour out my Spirit on all people. / Your sons and daughters will prophesy, / your young men will see visions, / your old men will dream dreams" (Acts 2:17).
- Scoffers will mock Christians, asking why Christ hasn't returned yet (2 Pet. 3:3).
- The gospel will have been preached to all nations (Matt. 24:14).
- "False prophets will appear and perform great signs and miracles to deceive" (Matt. 24:24).
- "The sun will be darkened, / and the moon will not give its light; / the stars will fall from the sky" (Matt. 24:29).
- "Men will not put up with sound doctrine. Instead, to suit their own desires, they will gather around them a great number of teachers to say what their itching ears want to hear. They will turn their ears away from the truth and turn aside to myths" (2 Tim. 4:3–4).

❧ DEFINITIONS OF LOVE ❧

- Greater love has no one than this, that he lay down his life for his friends. (John 15:13)
- But God demonstrates his own love for us in this: While we were still sinners, Christ died for us. (Rom. 5:8)
- Love is patient, love is kind. It does not envy, it does not boast, it is not proud. It is not rude, it is not self-seeking, it is not easily angered, it keeps no record of wrongs. Love does not delight in evil but rejoices with the truth. It always protects, always trusts, always hopes, always perseveres. (1 Cor. 13:4–7)
- This is how we know what love is: Jesus Christ laid down his life for us. And we ought to lay down our lives for our brothers. (1 John 3:16)
- God is love. Whoever lives in love lives in God, and God in him. (1 John 4:16)
- Perfect love drives out fear. (1 John 4:18)
- This is love for God: to obey his commands. (1 John 5:3)

❈ WATER IN THE BIBLE ❈

Water into blood (Exod. 7:20) • Bitter water (Exod. 15:23) •
Quiet waters (Ps. 23:2) • Water of affliction (Isa. 30:20) • Water in
the desert (Isa. 32:2) • Water into wine (John 2:9) • Living water (John 4:10) •
Pure water (Heb. 10:22) • Water of life (Rev. 21:6)

❈ ISRAEL'S FESTIVALS ❈

Name of Festival	*Description*	*Reference*
Sabbath	A weekly rest for people and animals	Exodus 20:8–11
Passover	An annual observance for the people to remember Israel's deliverance from Egyptian bondage	Exodus 12
Unleavened Bread	An annual observance for the people to remember how God brought Israel's ancestors out of Egypt in a hurry	Numbers 28
Firstfruits	An annual observance that caused the Israelites to recognize the Lord's goodness to them in their growing season	Leviticus 23
Weeks (Pentecost)	An annual opportunity to express gratitude for the Lord's blessing when the crops are harvested	Numbers 28
Trumpets	An annual observance in which the Israelites presented themselves to the Lord	Numbers 29
Day of Atonement	An annual observance in which the priests and the people were absolved of their guilt	Leviticus 16
Tabernacles (Booths)	An annual observance in which the people camped out in shelters to recall their forty-year journey from Egypt to the Promised Land	Leviticus 23
Sacred Assembly	An annual observance in which the people commemorated the closing of the cycle of feasts	Numbers 29

❀ UNLIKELY HEROES ❀

If you've ever tried reading through the "begats" of the Bible, you've likely discovered that it is like wandering through a cemetery far from home. The tombstones bear unfamiliar names. Many are unpronounceable and most seem uninteresting. But every once in a while, you trip over a footnote that's like a headstone describing a fascinating biography.

Some unlikely heroes include:

- Gideon, the least member of the weakest clan of Manasseh, was used by God to lead an army of only three hundred men to defeat a much larger army of Midianites.
- Esther, a Jewish orphan who became queen in an anti-Semitic kingdom and saved her people from annihilation.
- Ruth, a Gentile widow from Moab who became the great-grandmother of King David.
- Mary of Bethany, who anointed Jesus's feet with perfume and her tears; Jesus said her story would be told wherever the gospel is preached.
- Simon of Cyrene, who was conscripted out of the blue from the crowd in Jerusalem to carry Jesus's cross. Many believe that his son subsequently became a follower of Jesus (see Mark 15:21; Rom. 16:13).
- Cornelius, who had a major impact on the spread of Christianity to the Gentile world.
- Paul's nephew, who overheard a plot to kill his uncle and blew the whistle so that Paul was transferred under tight security to a cell in Caesarea before the threat could be carried out.
- Onesimus, who ran away from Philemon only to meet up with the apostle Paul, who led him to Christ and sent him back to his master; Paul was convinced that this young man could do great things for the kingdom.

❀ FRUIT BOTH LITERAL AND METAPHORICAL ❀

Literal
- Figs (Jer. 24:1–3)
- Grapes (Deut. 23:24)
- Olives (Deut. 8:8)
- Pomegranates (Num. 13:23)
- Sycamore-figs (Amos 7:14)

Metaphorical
- Proof of an effective life that is grounded in God's laws (Ps. 1:3)
- A Christlike lifestyle (Matt. 7:16)
- The evidence of abiding in Christ (John 15:16)
- Fruit of the Spirit (Gal. 5:22–23)
- Praise—the fruit of lips (Heb. 13:15)

❋ JACOB'S CHILDREN AND THEIR MOTHERS ❋

Name	Mother
Reuben	Leah
Simeon	Leah
Levi	Leah
Judah	Leah
Dan	Bilhah, Rachel's servant
Naphtali	Bilhah, Rachel's servant
Gad	Zilpah, Leah's servant
Asher	Zilpah, Leah's servant
Issachar	Leah
Zebulun	Leah
Dinah	Leah
Joseph	Rachel
Benjamin	Rachel

❋ NAMES FOR GOD AND WHAT THEY MEAN ❋

Name in Hebrew	Meaning	Reference
Elohim	God	Genesis 1:1
Adonai	Lord	Malachi 1:14
Jehovah	I AM WHO I AM (sometimes translated YAHWEH or LORD in all capital letters)	Genesis 2:4
Jehovah-Maccaddeshem	The Lord is your sanctifier	Exodus 31:13
Jehovah-Rohi	The Lord is my shepherd	Psalm 23:1
Jehovah-Shammah	The Lord who is present	Ezekiel 48:35
Jehovah-Rapha	The Lord who heals	Exodus 15:26
Jehovah-Tsidkenu	The Lord is our righteousness	Jeremiah 23:6
Jehovah-Jireh	The Lord will provide	Genesis 22:14
Jehovah-Nissi	The Lord is our banner	Exodus 17:15
Jehovah-Shalom	The Lord is our peace	Judges 6:24
Jehovah-Sabbaoth	The Lord of hosts	Isaiah 6:1
El-Elyon	The most high God	Genesis 14:18
El-Roi	The strong one who sees	Genesis 16:13
El-Shaddai	The Lord God Almighty	Psalm 91:1
El-Olam	The everlasting God	Isaiah 40:28

❧ FACTS ABOUT DEMONS ❧

They have names (Mark 5:9).

They can possess people (John 10:21).

They are under the authority of Beelzebub, or Satan (Matt. 12:24).

They can cause seizures (Luke 9:39).

They can cripple people (Luke 13:11).

They can prevent people from speaking (Luke 11:14).

They can give people extraordinary strength (Mark 5:4).

They can give people powers of divination (Acts 16:16).

Jesus was accused of being possessed (Matt. 9:34).

When exorcised, they can seek to possess someone else (Luke 11:24–26).

They can be exorcized by those who command them
to leave in Jesus's name (Mark 9:38).

Mary Magdalene had seven demons driven from her (Mark 16:9).

❧ REFERENCES TO JESUS IN THE PSALMS ❧

Reference in Psalms	*Reference to Christ*
Psalm 2:7	Jesus will be God's Son.
Psalm 16:8–10	Jesus will rise from the dead.
Psalm 22:1–18	Jesus will suffer on the cross.
Psalm 22:15	Jesus will thirst while on the cross.
Psalm 22:22	Jesus will declare God's name.
Psalm 34:20	Jesus's bones will not be broken.
Psalm 40:6–8	Jesus came to do God's will.
Psalm 41:9	Jesus will be betrayed.
Psalm 45:6–7	Jesus's throne will last forever.
Psalm 68:18	Jesus will ascend into heaven.
Psalm 69:9	Jesus has a passion for God.
Psalm 69:21	Jesus will become thirsty while on the cross and will be offered vinegar to drink.
Psalm 96:13	Jesus will one day return and judge the world.
Psalm 110:1	Jesus will be David's son and David's Lord.
Psalm 110:4	Jesus will be an eternal priest.
Psalm 118:22	Jesus will be rejected by many people.

❀ FOURTEEN KISSES ❀

- Jacob kissed his father Isaac deceitfully (Gen. 27:27).
- Jacob kissed Rachel when he was first introduced to her (Gen. 29:11).
- Esau kissed Jacob as a sign of reconciliation (Gen. 33:4).
- Joseph kissed his brothers as an expression of forgiveness (Gen. 45:15).
- Jacob kissed his two grandchildren good-bye when he was dying (Gen. 48:10).
- Moses kissed his brother Aaron (Exod. 4:27).
- Naomi kissed Ruth and Orpah (Ruth 1:9).
- Samuel kissed Saul at his coronation (1 Sam. 10:1).
- David kissed Jonathan in an expression of friendship (1 Sam. 20:41).
- David kissed his son Absalom after the boy's return (2 Sam. 14:33).
- A woman longed for her beloved's kiss (Song of Songs 1:2).
- A harlot kissed Jesus's feet (Luke 7:45).
- Judas kissed Jesus as he betrayed him (Matt. 26:49).
- The Ephesian elders kissed Paul as he departed (Acts 20:37).

❀ THE MOST INTENSE QUESTIONS ❀ ASKED IN THE BIBLE

- "But what about you?" he asked. "Who do you say I am?" Peter answered, "The Christ of God." (Luke 9:20)
- Then the LORD God said to the woman, "What is this you have done?" The woman said, "The serpent deceived me, and I ate." (Gen. 3:13)
- "What do you think about the Christ? Whose son is he?" "The son of David," they replied. (Matt. 22:42)
- Moses said to God, "Suppose I go to the Israelites and say to them, 'The God of your fathers has sent me to you,' and they ask me, 'What is his name?' Then what shall I tell them?" God said to Moses, "I AM WHO I AM. This is what you are to say to the Israelites: 'I AM has sent me to you.'" (Exod. 3:13–14)
- They all asked, "Are you then the Son of God?" He replied, "You are right in saying I am." (Luke 22:70)
- What good is it for a man to gain the whole world, yet forfeit his soul? (Mark 8:36)
- And at the ninth hour Jesus cried out in a loud voice, *"Eloi, Eloi, lama sabachthani?"*—which means, "My God, my God, why have you forsaken me?" (Mark 15:34)
- What good is it, my brothers, if a man claims to have faith but has no deeds? Can such faith save him? (James 2:14)

❀ THE GREATEST SAINTS AND THEIR SINS ❀

Before they became known as saints, Bible heroes were sinners like the rest of us. They even sinned as saints. These notable people in the Bible were not saints because of their stellar character traits but because of what God did through them. They were both remarkable and fallible. Consider:

Saint	Success	Failure
Adam	First created man	He disobeyed God.
Noah	A righteous man who obeyed God, built the ark, and kept the human race alive during the Flood	He got drunk on the grapes he grew in his vineyard.
Abraham	A man of faith who left his homeland at God's invitation yet was unsure where God was leading	He did not wait for God to make good on his promise of a son and had a child with his wife's servant.
Moses	Stood up to Pharaoh and successfully led God's people out of slavery in Egypt	He murdered an Egyptian early in his life. He also exhibited anger while shepherding the Israelites through the wilderness.
David	Killed the Philistine giant as a teen. As an adult became Israel's greatest king and was known as a man after God's own heart	He committed adultery with Bathsheba and then had her husband murdered.
Solomon	Succeeded his father, David, as Israel's king and built a temple for the worship of God	He disobeyed the Lord by marrying pagan wives and worshiping their gods.
Peter	Made public confession that Jesus was the Messiah and helped the Jerusalem church become established after Jesus's ascension	In spite of boasting that he was more loyal than his fellow disciples, he publicly denied that he knew Jesus three times.

❧ BIBLICAL TOPOGRAPHY ❧

- Deserts (Exod. 16:2)
- Plateaus (Josh. 13:16)
- Green pastures (Ps. 23:2)
- Mountains (Ps. 125:2)
- Valleys (Isa. 22:7)
- Ocean (Ps. 148:7)
- Rivers (Dan. 10:4)
- Fields (Exod. 10:5)
- Vineyards (Job 24:6)
- Olive groves (Neh. 9:25)
- Brooks (1 Kings 17:4)
- Gardens (Num. 24:6)
- Springs (1 Kings 18:5)
- Ravines (Ezek. 36:6)
- Gorges (Josh. 13:9)
- Seas (Deut. 3:17)
- Forests (2 Sam. 18:6)
- Caves (Judg. 6:2)
- Islands (Isa. 23:2)

❧ THE SUFFERINGS OF CHRIST ❧

In his movie *The Passion of the Christ*, Mel Gibson made millions portraying the horrendous torture Jesus underwent leading up to and on the cross. But long before Hollywood, the Bible showed us a moving picture that would be R-rated due to graphic violence.

Psalm 22 prophesies about Jesus's being forsaken by God the Father. In addition to the spiritual suffering Jesus endured while separated from God, the psalm points to the agony he felt hanging on the cross with his bones out of joint, his overworked heart feeling like wax, his strength sapped, his tongue dried to the roof of his mouth; all the while he watched people roll dice for his clothes and heard others pepper him with verbal insults.

The prophet Isaiah also weighed in on his sufferings. He pictured Jesus as a "man of sorrows" and acquainted with grief. He was despised and rejected, smitten, afflicted, pierced, and led "like a lamb to the slaughter" (Isa. 53:3, 7).

By the time you get to the scenes of suffering in the New Testament, it's as if they are projected in slow motion. Jesus is scourged with glass-tipped whips to within an inch of his life. He's pummeled with angry fists after being spat upon by a mob of soldiers who mock him. A crown of thorns is crushed on his head before he is forced to carry a seventy-five-pound crossbeam. Due to the extreme beatings he has received, he is unable to carry the crossbeam all the way to his execution. Simon of Cyrene carries the crossbeam behind an exhausted Jesus, who walks up the hill to where he is nailed to a cross. Each of the four Gospels (Matthew, Mark, Luke, and John) contributes pieces to the graphic yet glorious account of Jesus's death. The story seen in the New Testament is a perfect (yet sobering) overlay of the one in the Old Testament.

❧ NEHEMIAH'S INCREDIBLE PERSISTENCE ❧

Nehemiah led the endeavor to rebuild the walls of Jerusalem. He met with strong resistance from all sides.

Resistance	Nehemiah's Response	Reference
Sanballat and Tobiah angrily mocked Nehemiah.	Nehemiah and the people spent time in prayer and doubled their efforts to work.	Nehemiah 4:1–6
Sanballat, Tobiah, and a group of Arabs, Ammonites, and Ashdodites threatened to attack.	Nehemiah and the people spent time in prayer and appointed someone to guard at all times.	Nehemiah 4:7–9
The Israelites were discouraged and afraid.	Nehemiah reassured them and armed the workers.	Nehemiah 4:10–23
Some Jewish officials treated the poor badly by charging high interest rates and taking away their property.	Nehemiah rebuked the officials who did this and made them return the seized assets.	Nehemiah 5:1–13
Sanballat, Tobiah, and Geshem attempted to distract Nehemiah by offering to meet and talk with him.	Nehemiah refused their offers and stayed focused on finishing the walls.	Nehemiah 6:1–4
Sanballat spread rumors that Nehemiah wanted to become the king.	Nehemiah denied the rumors and prayed that God would give him strength.	Nehemiah 6:5–9

❧ MOVIE TITLES TAKEN FROM SCRIPTURE ❧

East of Eden • The Ten Commandments • King of Kings • The Last Temptation of Christ • David • The Robe • The Greatest Story Ever Told • The Passion of the Christ • The Bible • Ben Hur • King David

❋ THE MIRACLES OF JESUS ❋

During his three-year ministry, Jesus

- turned water into wine (John 2:1–9).
- healed the nobleman's son (John 4:46–53).
- exorcized the demoniac in Capernaum (Mark 1:23–26; Luke 4:33–35).
- healed Peter's mother-in-law (Matt. 8:14–15; Mark 1:29–31; Luke 4:38–39).
- supernaturally enabled a huge catch of fish (Luke 5:4–6; John 21:4–6).
- healed a leper (Matt. 8:1–4; Mark 1:40–44; Luke 5:12–14).
- healed a paralytic (Matt. 9:6–7; Mark 2:10–12; Luke 5:24–26).
- healed a man with a withered hand (Matt. 12:9–14; Mark 3:1–6; Luke 6:6–11)
- healed a centurion's servant (Matt. 8:5–13; Luke 7:1–10)
- raised a widow's son from the dead (Luke 7:14–15).
- commanded a stormy sea to become tranquil (Matt. 8:23–26; Mark 4:35–40; Luke 8:22–25).
- exorcized the Gadarene demoniac (Matt. 8:28–34; Mark 5:1–17; Luke 8:26–37).
- healed the woman with a blood disorder (Matt. 9:20–22; Mark 5:25–34; Luke 8:43–48).
- raised Jairus's daughter from the grave (Matt. 9:18–26; Mark 5:22–42; Luke 8:41–55).
- healed two blind men (Matt. 9:29–30).
- healed a dumb demoniac (Matt. 9:32–33).
- healed an invalid (John 5:8–9).
- fed five thousand people with a small lunch (Matt. 14:15–21; Mark 6:35–44; Luke 9:12–17; John 6:5–13).
- walked on the Sea of Galilee (Matt. 14:22–33; Mark 6:45–51; John 6:16–21).
- healed a girl possessed by demons (Matt. 15:21–28; Mark 7:24–30).
- healed a man with a speech impediment who was also deaf (Mark 7:34–35).
- fed four thousand people with a handful of food (Matt. 15:32–38; Mark 8:2–9).
- healed a blind man in the village of Bethsaida (Mark 8:22–25).
- healed a man blind from birth (John 9:1–7).
- healed a boy possessed by demons (Matt. 17:14–18; Mark 9:14–27; Luke 9:37–42).
- caused Peter to catch a fish with a coin in its mouth (Matt. 17:24–27).
- healed a blind and dumb demoniac (Luke 11:14).
- healed a woman with an eighteen-year illness (Luke 13:10–13).
- healed a man suffering from dropsy (Luke 14:1–4).
- healed ten men with leprosy (Luke 17:11–14).
- raised Lazarus from the dead (John 11:38–44).
- healed the blind man of Jericho (Matt. 20:29–34; Mark 10:46–52; Luke 18:35–43).
- caused the unfruitful fig tree to wither (Matt. 21:18–19; Mark 11:12–14, 20–21).
- restored a severed ear (Luke 22:50–51).

❀ THE PROMISES OF JESUS ❀

- But seek first his kingdom and his righteousness, and all these things will be given to you as well. (Matt. 6:33)

- Again, I tell you that if two of you on earth agree about anything you ask for, it will be done for you by my Father in heaven. (Matt. 18:19)

- For where two or three come together in my name, there am I with them. (Matt. 18:20).

- I will not leave you as orphans. (John 14:18)

- I am with you always, to the very end of the age. (Matt. 28:20)

- For everyone who exalts himself will be humbled, and he who humbles himself will be exalted. (Luke 18:14)

- You will receive power when the Holy Spirit comes on you; and you will be my witnesses. (Acts 1:8)

- Everyone who has left houses or brother or sister or father or mother or children or fields for my sake will receive a hundred times as much and will inherit eternal life. (Matt. 19:29)

- Give and it will be given to you. (Luke 6:38)

- Come unto me, all you who are weary and burdened, and I will give you rest. (Matt. 11:28)

- If they persecuted me, they will persecute you also. (John 15:20)

- I am going there to prepare a place for you. And if I go and prepare a place for you, I will come back and take you to be with me that you also may be where I am. (John 14:2–3)

- I tell you the truth, anyone who has faith in me will do what I have been doing. He will do even greater things than these, because I am going to the Father. (John 14:12)

- I will build my church, and the gates of Hades will not overcome it. (Matt. 16:18)

- In this world you will have trouble. (John 16:33)

- For everyone who asks receives; he who seeks finds; and to him who knocks, the door will be opened. (Luke 11:10)

- I tell you, whoever acknowledges me before men, the Son of Man will also acknowledge him before the angels of God. (Luke 12:8)

- For God so loved the world that he gave his one and only Son, that whoever believes in him shall not perish but have eternal life. (John 3:16)

- I am the resurrection and the life. He who believes in me will live, even though he dies. (John 11:25)

- I tell you the truth, anyone who gives you a cup of water in my name because you belong to Christ will certainly not lose his reward. (Mark 9:41)

❀ DEPRESSED ANONYMOUS ❀

Person	Evidence	Reference
Job	Why did I not perish at birth / and die as I came from the womb?	Job 3:11
Sons of Korah	My soul is downcast within me.	Psalm 42:6
Solomon	So my heart began to despair over all my toilsome labor under the sun.	Ecclesiastes 2:20
Elijah	I am the only one left, and now they are trying to kill me too.	1 Kings 19:14
Jeremiah	My eyes fail from weeping. / I am in torment within.	Lamentations 2:11
John the Baptist	Are you the one who is to come, or should we expect someone else?	Luke 7:20
Cleopas and another disciple	They stood still, their faces downcast.	Luke 24:17

❀ SURPRISING CONVERSIONS ❀

Person Converted	Surprising Circumstances	Reference
Abraham	Coming from a land and a family that worshiped other gods, he followed the call of God to move to Canaan and to serve only God.	Genesis 12:1–8
Nicodemus	Even though he was a Pharisee (a group who resisted Jesus), he came to the rabbi at night with a spiritual thirst.	John 3; 7:50–51; 19:38–40
Samaritan woman	Although this woman had been married several times and was currently living in sin, she responded to Jesus's overture of love, acceptance, and forgiveness.	John 4
Simon of Cyrene	This visitor to Jerusalem from out of the country was forced to carry Jesus's cross to Golgotha, but in the process began a relationship with him and passed his faith on to his two sons.	Mark 15; Romans 16:13
Thief on the cross	This criminal, who was crucified next to Jesus, recognized his divinity and called out to him for forgiveness before he died.	Luke 23
Ethiopian eunuch	Although this government envoy was intrigued by what he read in the scroll of Isaiah, he didn't understand it until Philip explained it to him on a desert road. The eunuch's unexpected confession of faith resulted in an unplanned baptism in the middle of nowhere.	Acts 8
Paul	This outspoken critic of Christianity was knocked off his high horse while riding to Damascus to imprison Jesus's followers. To the surprise of all who knew him, Paul surrendered his life to Christ.	Acts 9
Onesimus	This runaway slave found his way to Rome and ended up encountering Paul, who was under house arrest. Their friendship resulted in the slave's conversion and subsequent return to his owner.	Philemon 10

❃ THE SUFFERINGS OF PAUL ❃

Struck with temporary blindness (Acts 9:9)
Threatened with death in Damascus (Acts 9:24) and in Jerusalem (Acts 23:12)
Rejected by leaders of the Jerusalem church (Acts 9:26)
Lived with a lifelong ailment God refused to take away (2 Cor. 12:7–8)
Imprisoned on several occasions (Acts 16; 23–25)
Flogged (Acts 16:23)
Five times received thirty-nine lashes (2 Cor. 11:24)
Three times beaten with rods (2 Cor. 11:25)
Stoned (Acts 14:19)
Shipwrecked three times (2 Cor. 11:25)
Betrayed by Peter (Gal. 2)
Abandoned by John Mark (Acts 15:37–39)

❃ UNIQUE AND UNUSUAL DEATHS ❃

- Lot's wife disobeyed the warning not to look back at Sodom and Gomorrah as her family fled for their lives, and she became a pillar of salt (Gen. 19:26).
- The firstborn of people and animals of the Egyptians were slain when the angel of death passed over Egypt (Exod. 11–12).
- When Korah, Dathan, and Abiram incited the Israelites to challenge Moses's leadership in the wilderness, the ground opened up and swallowed them alive (Num. 16:32).
- When Eli the priest heard that his sons were among those who had died in battle against the Philistines, he fell backward off his chair and broke his neck (1 Sam. 4:18).
- While attempting to steal his father's throne, King David's son Absalom died when his signature long, flowing hair got caught in a tree and Joab stabbed him to death (2 Sam. 18:9, 14).
- Haman was hung on the very gallows he'd had built to execute Mordecai (Esther 7:10).
- Eighteen men from Jerusalem died when the Tower of Siloam collapsed and fell on them (Luke 13:4).
- After betraying Jesus into the hands of the bloodthirsty chief priests, Judas had such remorse he hanged himself (Matt. 27:5).
- Ananias and Sapphira each collapsed and died on the spot when they were confronted with their deceit (Acts 5).
- King Herod received the praise of his subjects, who called him a god, and when he did not acknowledge the Lord, he died as the result of being devoured by worms (Acts 12:23).

❊ HYMNS FROM SCRIPTURE ❊

The ancient followers of God sang sections of Scripture as hymns. Included with each reference is a small sampling of the hymn:

Exodus 15:1–18

> I will sing to the LORD,
> > for he is highly exalted.
>
> The horse and its rider
> > he has hurled into the sea.
>
> The LORD is my strength and my song;
> > he has become my salvation.
>
> He is my God, and I will praise him,
> > my father's God, and I will exalt him. (vv. 1–2)

Psalm 100:1–5

> Shout for joy to the LORD, all the earth.
> Worship the LORD with gladness;
> > come before him with joyful songs.
>
> Know that the LORD is God.
> > It is he who made us, and we are his;
>
> we are his people, the sheep of his pasture. (vv. 1–3)

Psalm 150:1–6

> Praise the LORD.
> Praise God in his sanctuary;
> > praise him in his mighty heavens.
>
> Praise him for his acts of power. (vv. 1–2)

❊ IMPERSONATORS MENTIONED IN THE BIBLE ❊

- Jacob disguised himself as his brother, Esau (Gen. 27).

- Tamar disguised herself as a prostitute (Gen. 38).

- Saul disguised himself while visiting the witch of Endor (1 Sam. 28).

- Jesus disguised himself as a stranger on the road to Emmaus (Luke 24:13–35).

- Wolves (false teachers) disguise themselves as sheep (Matt. 7:15).

- Satan disguises himself as an angel of light (2 Cor. 11:14).

❧ PERSONS INVOLVED IN THE PASSION OF CHRIST ❧

Person	Description	Reference
Jesus	Betrayed, beaten, mocked, and crucified.	Luke 22–23
Judas Iscariot	Betrayed Jesus for thirty pieces of silver and later committed suicide.	Luke 22:1–6; Matthew 27:3–5
Peter	Denied he knew Jesus during the interrogation.	Luke 22:54–62
Caiaphas	High priest who sat in judgment over Jesus and accused him of blasphemy.	Matthew 26:57–68
Pontius Pilate	Reluctantly gave in to the mob's request that Jesus be crucified.	Luke 22:66–23:25
Herod	Joined with his soldiers in mocking Jesus as a king but found no reason to have Jesus killed.	Luke 23:6–12
Simon of Cyrene	Forced by the Romans to carry Jesus's cross when the condemned rabbi fell under its weight.	Mark 15:21
Two thieves	One mocked Jesus and died a cynic; the other acknowledged his life of sin and, recognizing the divinity of Jesus, asked for forgiveness.	Luke 23:39–43
The centurion	Stood at the foot of the cross and observed the way Jesus died. When it was all over, he was convinced he'd been in the presence of the Son of God.	Luke 23:47

❧ THE UNLIKELY ANCESTORS OF THE MESSIAH ❧

Jesus was purebred, right? Well, he was virgin-born. His earthly mother was highly favored by the Most High. He was born without sin. He lived a perfect life. But if you dig around in some of the closets of his ancestors, you might be surprised at what you uncover. Tamar seduced her father-in-law and became pregnant by him (Gen. 38). Rahab was a harlot from Jericho (Josh. 2). Ruth was a Gentile from the uncircumcised nation of Moab (Ruth 1). David was an adulterer and a murderer (2 Sam. 11). Ahaz was a king who worshiped Baal (2 Chron. 28). There are a whole lot more, but suffice it to say the One born to bear the sin of the world did his share of bearing the sin of his extended family.

❈ A BIBLICAL WINE LIST ❈

- Samson observed the Nazirite vow that forbade drinking wine, but he made other choices that were anything but godly (Judg. 13:14).
- The psalmist found that wine in responsible amounts can be a joy enhancer (Ps. 104:15).
- King Solomon warned his subjects that wine can cause those who imbibe to become mockers (Prov. 20:1).
- According to the Proverbs, irresponsible consumption of wine leads to sorrow, strife, and physical problems (Prov. 23:29–30).
- The bride of Solomon knew how wonderful a cup of wine was and yet said her husband's love was far more delightful (Song of Songs 1:2).
- Daniel and his Hebrew friends refused to drink wine so as not to become defiled by the pagan culture in which they found themselves (Dan. 1:8).
- Jesus knew the importance of having enough wine at a special occasion and supernaturally transformed jugs of water into wine in order to save the host embarrassment (John 2:9).
- Jesus infused a cup of Passover wine with new meaning when he said, "This is my blood of the [new] covenant" (Matt. 26:28).
- The apostle Paul warned first-century Christians that drinking wine to excess leads to debauchery (Eph. 5:18).
- The apostle Paul was convinced that a little wine is good for stomach problems (1 Tim. 5:23).

❈ NAKED RUNNERS IN THE BIBLE ❈

Streaking blurred the lines of propriety back in the seventies when college students ran through hallways and across campuses in nothing more than their birthday suits. Administrators blushed with embarrassment because the naked truth was they hadn't anticipated such antics, and their policy manuals failed to specifically address such behavior. In other words, they'd failed to cover their behinds.

Nonetheless, running in the nude was not new in the decade that followed the peace and love movement of the sixties. For three years the Old Testament Isaiah walked around *without shoes or clothes* as a way of illustrating the message God had given him to share with Israel (Isa. 20:3). Another streaker in the Bible (who ran instead of walking) was Mark, the young friend of Jesus who would eventually write a Gospel. When Jesus was arrested in the Garden of Gethsemane, Mark was in attendance. As soldiers attempted to seize him, they grabbed his linen garment, but the young man slipped out of it and ran away totally exposed (Mark 14:51).

❀ GODLESS SONS OF GODLY FATHERS ❀

Godless Son	Godly Father
Rehoboam	Solomon
Jehoram	Jehoshaphat
Ahaz	Jotham
Manasseh	Hezekiah
Jehoahaz	Josiah

❀ METAPHORS FOR THE CHURCH ❀

Expression	Meaning	Reference
The Way	Those who belong to Christ understand that he is the way to God, and thus their shared journey of faith is "the Way."	Acts 24:14
God's Household	Those joined together by a common faith are like a family. God is their Father and they are brothers and sisters in Christ.	Ephesians 2:19
The Family of Believers	Those who are joined together by a common faith are like a family. God is their Father and they are brothers and sisters in Christ.	Galatians 6:10
The Body of Christ	Christ is the head of the church and each member is like a different body part or organ that contributes a necessary function.	1 Corinthians 12:12–27
God's Flock	Jesus identified himself as the Good Shepherd. As such, Peter picked up on this metaphor and referred to Christians as those under his care who are within the fold.	1 Peter 5:2
The Bride of Christ	The church is the object of Jesus's love. Having laid down his life for her, he commits himself to her in a binding covenant.	Revelation 19:7–9

❈ BELIEVE IT OR NOT ❈

- Enoch never died. As a reward for walking with God, "God took him away" (Gen. 5).

- As she was fleeing Sodom and Gomorrah, Lot's wife looked back and was transformed into a pillar of salt (Gen. 19).

- At the end of his life, the prophet Elijah didn't die. Rather, he was carried away in a chariot that disappeared from earth in a whirlwind (2 Kings 2).

- When Jonah resisted his assignment from the Lord, he booked passage on a ship headed in the opposite direction from where he'd been sent. During a storm, he was thrown overboard and swallowed by a large fish. Amazingly, he survived for three days before being spewed up on a beach (Jon. 1–2).

- The fingers of a human hand appeared and began to write on a plaster wall in the palace of Babylon, which caused King Belshazzar to pale with fright (Dan. 5).

- Mary became pregnant without having had sexual intercourse (Luke 1).

- Jesus turned jars of drinking water into wine at a wedding party in Cana (John 2).

- Jesus appeared alive to as many as five hundred people after being crucified, pronounced dead, and buried for three days (1 Cor. 15).

- One hundred twenty followers of Jesus gathered in an upper room in Jerusalem during the Festival of Pentecost. The sound of a gale-force wind filled the room and individual flames of fire appeared over each person. Then, as they praised God, they began to speak in languages they had never learned. As it turned out, the languages being spoken were the same languages of the visitors to Jerusalem who stood nearby and heard them (Acts 2).

- Paul, a card-carrying Pharisee, was known for his hatred toward Christians. He consented to their deaths and went out of his way to lock them up in jail. Amazingly, after a life-changing encounter with Jesus he had a change of heart and became the most enthusiastic advocate for Christianity in the Roman Empire (Acts 9).

❈ FAMOUS QUARRELS ❈

- Cain and Abel (Gen. 4:8)
- Abram's herdsmen and Lot's herdsmen (Gen. 13:7)
- Jacob and Esau (Gen. 27:41)
- Saul and David (1 Sam. 18:9)
- Martha and Mary (Luke 10:40)
- Between the disciples (Luke 22:24)
- Paul and Barnabas (Acts 15:37–39)
- Paul and Peter (Gal. 2:11)
- Euodia and Syntyche (Phil. 4:2)

❊ VARIOUS ALTARS FOUND IN THE BIBLE ❊

Altar erected by	Location	Reference
Noah	Mount Ararat	Genesis 8:20
Abraham	Shechem	Genesis 12:7
Abraham	Hebron	Genesis 13:18
Abraham	Moriah	Genesis 22:9
Isaac	Beersheba	Genesis 26:25
Jacob	Shechem	Genesis 33:20
Jacob	Bethel	Genesis 35:1–7
Moses	Rephidim	Exodus 17:15
Balak	Bamoth Baal	Numbers 23:1
Joshua	Mount Ebal	Joshua 8:30
Tribes living east of the Jordan River	Geliloth	Joshua 22:10
Gideon	Ophrah	Judges 6:24
Manoah	Zorah	Judges 13:20
Israel	Bethel	Judges 21:4
Samuel	Ramah	1 Samuel 7:17
Saul	Aijalon	1 Samuel 14:35
David	Threshing floor of Araunah	2 Samuel 24:25
Jeroboam	Bethel	1 Kings 12:32
Ahab	Samaria	1 Kings 16:32
Elijah	Mount Carmel	1 Kings 18:32
Uriah	Jerusalem	2 Kings 16:11
Zerubbabel	Jerusalem	Ezra 3:2

❊ THE MAN WITH SIX FINGERS ❊

To say someone is "all thumbs" means that he is clumsy. But what would you call someone who had six fingers on each hand and six toes on each foot? Digitally enhanced? The Bible calls such a person *huge*! "In still another battle, which took place at Gath, there was a huge man with six fingers on each hand and six toes on each foot—twenty-four in all" (2 Sam. 21:20). You couldn't very well give such a person a high-five. You'd give him a high-six.

❈ CLOSE ENCOUNTERS IN THE TEMPLE ❈

Have you ever sung the praise song "We Are Standing on Holy Ground"? Just voicing the words is a reminder that the sanctuary is more than a shelter. It's a sacred space where we expect to encounter God. In both the Old and the New Testaments, individuals were aware that the temple was not an ordinary hangout.

The prophet Isaiah, for example, was blown away by a vision of the Lord in the temple. The sight he described (Isa. 6) is almost enough to give a grown man nightmares. Flying angel-like creatures deposited burning coals on his tongue (perhaps that's where your mom got the idea to wash your mouth out with soap when she heard you cut loose with a curse word).

In the New Testament, Zechariah encountered Gabriel the angel during his shift in the temple (Luke 1). Once he got over the shock of being visited by an angel, Zechariah heard Gabriel say that he and his barren bride (both past midlife) were going to be parents. When he scoffed at the suggestion, Zechariah was unable to speak for more than nine months.

And then there are the encounters with Jesus in the temple. First, as a boy of twelve he stumped the elders with his uncanny insights (Luke 2). As a man of thirty-three he rearranged the moneychangers' furniture in the temple without being asked (Matt. 21).

❈ EARTHQUAKES IN THE BIBLE ❈

- In the Sinai desert when God gave the Law (Exod. 19:18)

- While Elijah was standing on a mountain (1 Kings 19:11)

- In Jerusalem while Uzziah was king (Zech. 14:5)

- In Jerusalem at the time Jesus was crucified (Matt. 27:54)

- In Jerusalem on the morning of the Resurrection (Matt. 28:2)

- In Philippi while Paul and Silas were in prison (Acts 16:26)

- The earthquakes that are part of living in an imperfect world subject to the natural disasters on planet Earth (Ps. 46:2–3)

- The earthquakes that will signal the end of time (Matt. 24:7)

- The earthquakes that will be felt on earth during the Tribulation in the last days when the sixth seal is opened (Rev. 6:12), when the seventh seal is opened (Rev. 8:5), at the raising of the two witnesses (Rev. 11:13), and at the pouring out of the vial at Armageddon (Rev. 16:17–18)

❊ THE "I AM" STATEMENTS OF JESUS ❊

Statement	Meaning	Reference
"I am the bread of life."	In him the spiritually hungry are fed.	John 6:35
"I am the light of the world."	He illuminates truth.	John 8:12
"I am the door."	Jesus is the means by which we enter into the presence of a holy God.	John 10:9 (KJV)
"I am the good shepherd."	He seeks those who are lost and upon finding them, cares for them.	John 10:11
"I am the resurrection and the life."	Because of his power over death (as demonstrated in his ability to rise from the grave), those who believe in him will also rise.	John 11:25
"I am the way and the truth and the life."	Jesus is the only means by which human beings can experience a relationship with their Creator.	John 14:6
"I am the true vine."	Being connected to Jesus is the only means of experiencing spiritual life and bearing fruit.	John 15:1

❊ METAPHORS FOR GOD'S PROTECTION ❊

- A rock and fortress (Ps. 18:2)
- A shepherd caring for his sheep (Ps. 23)
- An impenetrable fortress for people at risk (Ps. 46)
- A bird who spreads his wings over his brood (Ps. 91:4)
- A mother bear protecting her young (Hos. 13:8)

❊ PRECIOUS GEMSTONES ❊

Kind of Stone	Reference
Onyx	Exodus 39
Ruby	Exodus 39
Agate	Exodus 39
Turquoise	Exodus 39
Carbuncle	Isaiah 54 (KJV)
Coral	Job 28:18
Diamond	Jeremiah 17:1 (KJV)
Jasper	Revelation 21
Sapphire	Revelation 21
Chalcedony	Revelation 21
Emerald	Revelation 21
Sardonyx	Revelation 21 (KJV)
Carnelian	Revelation 21
Chrysolyte	Revelation 21 (KJV)
Beryl	Revelation 21
Topaz	Revelation 21
Chrysoprase	Revelation 21
Jacinth	Revelation 21
Amethyst	Revelation 21
Pearl	Revelation 21

❊ JESUS'S TEACHINGS ABOUT CHILDREN ❊

- ▦ He taught that God is even more inclined to respond to individual's needs than an earthly father is inclined to respond to a child's genuine need (Luke 11:11).
- ▦ He taught that people must become like little children in order to experience the kingdom of God (Matt. 18:3).
- ▦ He taught by example that children are to be valued and honored as special (Luke 18:16).
- ▦ He taught that death is a just penalty for those who cause children to be misled or to stumble (Luke 17:2).
- ▦ He taught that God has revealed spiritual insights to "little children," his humble disciples, that he has hidden from religious authorities (Matt. 11:25).
- ▦ He taught that children have a built-in instinct to praise God (Matt. 21:16).

❈ CITY BUILDERS ❈

- Cain built a city and named it after his son Enoch (Gen. 4:17).
- Nimrod built Babylon, Erech, Akkad, and Calneh. In Assyria he built Nineveh, Rehoboth Ir, Calah, and Resen (Gen. 10:10–12).
- An unnamed man from Bethel built a city called Luz in the land of the Hittites (Judg. 1:26).
- Solomon "built up Lower Beth Horon, Baalath, and Tadmor in the desert, within his land, as well as all his store cities and the towns for his chariots and for his horses—whatever he desired to build in Jerusalem, in Lebanon and throughout all the territory he ruled" (1 Kings 9:17–19).
- Jeroboam fortified Shechem and Peniel (1 Kings 12:25).
- Omri built Samaria (1 Kings 16:24).
- Solomon fortified Upper Beth Horon, Lower Beth Horon, and Baalath (2 Chron. 8:4–6).
- Rehoboam built Bethlehem, Etam, Tekoa, Beth Zur, Soco, Adullam, Gath, Mareshah, Ziph, Adoraim, Lachish, Azekah, Zorah, Aijalon, and Hebron (2 Chron. 11:5–10).
- Jotham "built towns in the Judean hills and forts and towers in the wooded areas" (2 Chron. 27:4).

❈ WITCHES IN THE BIBLE ❈

A clean sweep of the Scriptures indicates only one person who was specifically identified as a witch, and even she did not have a broom. The witch of Endor was one who practiced sorcery. In 1 Samuel, King Saul, who forbade consultation with a medium, himself sought the advice of this witch. In the New Testament book of Acts, a man by the name of Simon Magnus dabbled in magic (Acts 8), which technically made him a male witch. In addition to these two individuals, both the Old and New Testaments contain references to witchcraft; for example, Micah 5:12; Nahum 3:4; and Galatians 5:19–20.

God's attitude toward witchcraft is evident in this text:

> Let no one be found among you who sacrifices his son or daughter in the fire, who practices divination or sorcery, interprets omens, engages in witchcraft, or casts spells, or who is a medium or spiritist or who consults the dead. Anyone who does these things is detestable to the LORD, and because of these detestable practices the LORD your God will drive out those nations before you. (Deut. 18:10–12)

❊ THE BOOKS OF THE BIBLE ACCORDING ❊
TO THEIR LITERARY GENRE

Book of the Bible	*Genre*
Genesis	Poetry/History
Exodus	History
Leviticus	History
Numbers	History
Deuteronomy	History
Joshua	History
Judges	History
Ruth	History
1 Samuel	History
2 Samuel	History
1 Kings	History
2 Kings	History
1 Chronicles	History
2 Chronicles	History
Ezra	History
Nehemiah	History
Esther	History
Job	Poetry
Psalms	Poetry
Proverbs	Poetry
Ecclesiastes	Poetry
Song of Solomon	Poetry
Isaiah	History/Prophecy
Jeremiah	History/Prophecy
Lamentations	History
Ezekiel	History/Prophecy
Daniel	History/Prophecy
Hosea	Prophecy
Joel	Prophecy
Amos	Prophecy
Obadiah	Prophecy
Jonah	Prophecy/Poetry
Micah	Prophecy

Book of the Bible	Genre
Nahum	Prophecy
Habakkuk	Prophecy
Zephaniah	Prophecy
Haggai	Prophecy
Zechariah	Prophecy
Malachi	Prophecy
Matthew	Interpretive History
Mark	Interpretive History
Luke	Interpretive History/Correspondence
John	Interpretive History
Acts	Interpretive History/Correspondence
Romans	Theology/Correspondence
1 Corinthians	Theology/Correspondence
2 Corinthians	Theology/Correspondence
Galatians	Theology/Correspondence
Ephesians	Theology/Correspondence
Philippians	Theology/Correspondence
Colossians	Theology/Correspondence
1 Thessalonians	Theology/Correspondence
2 Thessalonians	Theology/Correspondence
1 Timothy	Theology/Correspondence
2 Timothy	Theology/Correspondence
Titus	Theology/Correspondence
Philemon	Theology/Correspondence
Hebrews	Theology/Correspondence
James	Theology/Correspondence
1 Peter	Theology/Correspondence
2 Peter	Theology/Correspondence
1 John	Theology/Correspondence
2 John	Theology/Correspondence
3 John	Theology/Correspondence
Jude	Theology/Correspondence
Revelation	Prophecy/Apocalyptic

❄ NAMES THAT GOD CHANGED ❄

Many biblical figures had their names altered. Sometimes God arranged these changes and sometimes he declared them directly. These new names often reflected new roles, transformed character, or special honor. Changed names also give us clues about God's purposes in these people's lives. For example:

Old Name	New Name	Reference
Abram	Abraham	Genesis 17:5
Sarai	Sarah	Genesis 17:15
Jacob	Israel	Genesis 32:28
Daniel	Belteshazzar	Daniel 1:7
Hananiah	Shadrach	Daniel 1:7
Mishael	Meshach	Daniel 1:7
Azariah	Abednego	Daniel 1:7
Simon	Peter	Mark 3:16
Saul	Paul	Acts 13:9

❄ EUPHEMISMS FOR SEX ❄

Adam knew Eve his wife (Gen. 4:1 KJV).

[Abram] slept with Hagar (Gen. 16:4).

Defiled (Gen. 34:5).

Lie with (Lev. 18:22).

Stand before (Lev. 18:23 KJV).

He went to her (Ruth 4:13).

Wash your feet (2 Sam. 11:8).

Come to bed (2 Sam. 13:11).

Go in unto (2 Sam. 16:21 KJV).

Embrace the bosom (Prov. 5:20).

Drink deep of love (Prov. 7:18).

Give you my love (Song of Songs 7:12).

Be intimate with (Hos. 3:3).

Touch (1 Cor. 7:1 KJV).

Come together (1 Cor. 7:5).

❄ DEMONS VERSUS JESUS ❄
(WINNER BY A KNOCKOUT: JESUS)

- When evening came, many who were demon-possessed were brought to him, and he drove out the spirits with a word and healed all the sick. (Matt. 8:16)

- While they were going out, a man who was demon-possessed and could not talk was brought to Jesus. (Matt. 9:32)

- Then they brought him a demon-possessed man who was blind and mute, and Jesus healed him, so that he could both talk and see. (Matt. 12:22)

- Jesus rebuked the demon, and it came out of the boy, and he was healed from that moment. (Matt. 17:18)

- Just then a man in their synagogue who was possessed by an evil spirit cried out, "What do you want with us, Jesus of Nazareth? Have you come to destroy us? I know who you are—the Holy One of God!" (Mark 1:23–24)

- "Be quiet!" said Jesus sternly. "Come out of him!" The evil spirit shook the man violently and came out of him with a shriek. (Mark 1:25–26)

- The whole town gathered at the door, and Jesus healed many who had various diseases. He also drove out many demons, but he would not let the demons speak because they knew who he was. (Mark 1:33–34)

- Then he told her, "For such a reply, you may go; the demon has left your daughter." She went home and found her child lying on the bed, and the demon gone. (Mark 7:29–30)

- When Jesus stepped ashore, he was met by a demon-possessed man from the town. For a long time this man had not worn clothes or lived in a house, but had lived in the tombs. When he saw Jesus, he cried out and fell at his feet, shouting at the top of his voice, "What do you want with me, Jesus, Son of the Most High God? I beg you, don't torture me!" For Jesus had commanded the evil spirit to come out of the man. Many times it had seized him, and though he was chained hand and foot and kept under guard, he had broken his chains and had been driven by the demon into solitary places. Jesus asked him, "What is your name?" "Legion," he replied, because many demons had gone into him. (Luke 8:27–30)

❈ HOW TO SPOT A FALSE TEACHER ❈

The Bible instructs us to beware of false teachers. Here are a few ways we can spot who is real and who isn't:

They will deceive many . . . . "For false Christs and false prophets will appear and perform great signs and miracles to deceive even the elect—if that were possible" (Matt. 24:24).

They seek their own honor . . . . . "He who speaks on his own does so to gain honor for himself, but he who works for the honor of the one who sent him is a man of truth; there is nothing false about him" (John 7:18).

They preach a distorted Jesus . . . "For if someone comes to you and preaches a Jesus other than the Jesus we preached, or if you receive a different spirit from the one you received, or a different gospel from the one you accepted, you put up with it easily enough. . . . For such men are false apostles, deceitful workmen, masquerading as apostles of Christ" (2 Cor. 11:4, 13).

Their teaching enslaves . . . . "This matter arose because some false brothers
Christians had infiltrated our ranks to spy on the freedom we have in Christ Jesus and to make us slaves" (Gal. 2:4).

They introduce heresies . . . . "But there were also false prophets among the people, just as there will be false teachers among you. They will secretly introduce destructive heresies, even denying the sovereign Lord who bought them—bringing swift destruction on themselves" (2 Pet. 2:1).

They deny that Jesus took . . . . . "Dear friends, do not believe every spirit, but
on a human body test the spirits to see whether they are from God, because many false prophets have gone out into the world. This is how you can recognize the Spirit of God: Every spirit that acknowledges that Jesus Christ has come in the flesh is from God, but every spirit that does not acknowledge Jesus is not from God" (1 John 4:1–3).

❀ KINDS OF FASTING ❀

Until relatively recently, many considered fasting a basic spiritual discipline. Increased interest in dietary health has again focused attention on the benefits of deliberate limitations on eating and drinking. The Bible's lack of detail in describing the practice indicates that people in ancient times understood it. Fasting today requires both instruction and application. The following are motivating models:

Type of Fast	Occasion	Reference
A fast of spiritual sorrow	Moses fasted for forty days when Israel sinned.	Deuteronomy 9:9
A fast of personal sorrow	David fasted after Saul's death.	2 Samuel 1:12
A fast in an attempt to influence God's decision	David fasted while the child of his adulterous relationship with Bathsheba was sick.	2 Samuel 12:16
A fast of renewal	Elijah fasted for forty days after escaping from Jezebel.	1 Kings 19:8
A fast of humility	Ahab fasted before God to demonstrate his humility.	1 Kings 21:27
A fast of justice	Isaiah reminded the nation that the fasting God takes most pleasure in is the kind where his people put aside their appetites for personal wants in order to undo the wrongs of society.	Isaiah 58:6
A fast of intercession	Esther fasted as a way to communicate to God her desire that her people be delivered.	Esther 4:16
A fast of focus	Anna fasted for decades as she anticipated and waited for the coming Messiah.	Luke 2:37
A fast to obtain power for ministry	Jesus fasted for forty days prior to the beginning of his public ministry.	Matthew 4:2
A fast to obtain divine guidance	The elders in Antioch fasted before sending Paul and Barnabas out on assignment.	Acts 13:2

❃ SUPERNATURAL BATTLES ❃

- The Lord parted the Red Sea, letting the Hebrews through to escape the Egyptians. Then with the Egyptian army halfway across, the sea rushed back into place, drowning them (Exod. 14:13–31).

- Joshua's defense against the Amalekites depended on Moses's ability to keep his arms raised (Exod. 17:8–16).

- The Israelites shouted to collapse the walls of Jericho, allowing them to attack the city (Josh. 6:1–21).

- To help Joshua against the Amorites, the Lord threw large hailstones at them from heaven and then kept the sun up an extra day (Josh. 10:6–14).

- God sent thunder from heaven so loud that it threw the Philistines into a panic, and the Israelites killed them as they fled (1 Sam. 7:10–11).

- God sent an earthquake that caused such confusion among the Philistines that they started killing one another (1 Sam. 14:8–23).

- With a one-sentence prayer, Elisha struck blind the army of the king of Aram. The prophet led them into Israel's capital, restored their sight, and had the king of Israel give them a feast before sending them home without a fight (2 Kings 6:18–23).

- The Arameans hastily abandoned their siege of Samaria when God caused them to hear the sounds of an enormous army (2 Kings 7:6–7).

- The angel of the Lord repelled the Assyrian army in Isaiah's day by killing 185,000 of its soldiers during the night (2 Kings 19:35–36).

❃ THE BOLDEST MEN OF THE BIBLE ❃

- Moses stood up to Pharaoh and demanded that he free the Hebrews (Exod. 5).

- Joshua and Caleb countered the negative report of the ten spies after returning from a reconnaissance trek into the Promised Land (Num. 13).

- Daniel defied the king and continued to pray three times a day even though such behavior was against the law (Dan. 6).

- Peter and the other disciples stood up to the chief priests and said they had to obey God rather than any human (Acts 5).

- Stephen stood up to his critics and boldly proclaimed the message of salvation as they prepared to stone him to death (Acts 7).

❀ FAMOUS ROADS AND WHAT THEY'RE KNOWN FOR ❀

Road	Description	Reference
Main road through Edom	A highway that led from the wilderness to the Promised Land—the Israelites were not permitted to travel on it.	Numbers 20:19–21
The highway from Bethel to Shechem	A celebration took place along this road.	Judges 21:19
The highway from Ekron to Bethshemesh	The road the ark of the covenant traveled as it headed back to Israel from Philistia.	1 Samuel 6:12
The Millennial Highway	A stretch of road from Egypt to Assyria on which people from various nations will travel to worship God in Jerusalem at the end of time.	Isaiah 19:23
A highway for our God	A symbolic reference to the Almighty's entrance into our world.	Isaiah 40:3
The broad road	A symbolic picture of the way that leads to destruction that many will travel.	Matthew 7:13
The narrow road	A symbolic picture of the way that leads to life that few will travel.	Matthew 7:14
The road that led from Bethphage to Jerusalem	The road on which Jesus came into town on a donkey while the crowds waved palm branches.	Matthew 21:1–11
The Jericho road	A well-traveled highway that led from Jerusalem to Jericho and served as the backdrop for Jesus's famous parable about the good Samaritan.	Luke 10:30
The road from Jerusalem to Emmaus	The trail on which two disciples were walking when Jesus appeared to them, though they were unaware he had risen from the dead.	Luke 24:13–16
The Damascus road	The highway between Israel and Syria on which Saul was traveling when he encountered the risen Christ.	Acts 9:3
Straight Street	The street in Damascus where Ananias found Saul and prayed for him to receive his sight.	Acts 9:11

❧ GREAT SINS AND THEIR CONSEQUENCES ❧

- Adam and Eve disobeyed the Lord's injunction against eating fruit from the tree of the knowledge of good and evil. As a result, God banished them from Eden (Gen. 3).

- Abraham failed to trust God to fulfill his promise of giving him a son and had a child through a surrogate. As a result, an ethnic group came into being that has warred with the Israelites for centuries (Gen. 16).

- Moses angrily disobeyed the Lord by striking the rock in the wilderness twice instead of once. As a result, God denied him entrance into the Promised Land (Num. 20).

- David committed adultery with Bathsheba and then conspired to cover up his sin by having the woman's husband killed. As a result, the child of his affair with Bathsheba died (2 Sam. 12).

- Jonah ran away from God's call to go to Nineveh. As a result, Jonah was swallowed by a large fish until he changed his mind and decided to do what the Lord asked (Jon. 1–2).

- Ananias and Sapphira conspired to deceive the leaders of the Jerusalem church about the money they gave to charity. As a result, both of them died (Acts 5).

- After King Herod delivered an address to the people, they shouted, "This is the voice of a god, not of a man." Herod accepted the praise of the people and refused to honor God. Because of this, an angel immediately struck him down, and he was eaten by worms and died (Acts 12).

❧ REFERENCES TO SALT ❧

- Lot's wife became a pillar of salt when she looked back at Sodom and Gomorrah as she fled the twin cities God was judging (Gen. 19:26).

- Salt was used as an ingredient in offerings made to the Lord (Ezek. 43:24).

- Salt was added to a mixture in the incense that was burned before the Lord (Exod. 30:35).

- Jesus described his disciples as "the salt of the earth," inferring their indispensable role in preserving a decaying society (Matt. 5:13).

- The apostle Paul suggested that the conversations of Christians be seasoned with salt, implying that they be flavorful and tasty (Col. 4:6).

- The apostle James contrasted salt water and fresh water in making a case for not being hypocritical (James 3:12).

❋ UNUSUAL LIFE SPANS ❋

The first person of the human race was a long-distance liver. Adam lived to be 930 years of age (Gen. 5). Noah was still blowing out birthday candles at 950 years (Gen. 9). But a guy named Methuselah lived even longer than that. His body didn't shut down until he reached the milestone of 969 years (Gen. 5). Not only did his tombstone boast a rather long and difficult name to pronounce, it also indicated he held the record of living longer than anyone else on planet Earth. It's a record that has never been broken. By the time Moses was leading the Israelites through the wilderness toward the Promised Land, people weren't living as long. In Psalm 90 Moses admits that the average life span is 70 years, maybe even 80. And even with high-tech medical care, it's still about the same 3,000 years later.

❋ GIANTS BIG AND TALL ❋

Name	Description	Reference
Anak	Father of a race of giants that lived in Canaan	Deuteronomy 9:2
Sheshai, Ahiman, and Talmai	Anak's three sons whom Caleb conquered	Joshua 15:14
Sippai	A Philistine warrior who died at the hands of Israelite soldiers	1 Chronicles 20:4
Goliath	The Philistine champion who was over nine feet tall but who was killed by David's slingshot	1 Samuel 17
Lahmi	Goliath's brother who died in battle at the hands of an Israelite soldier	1 Chronicles 20:5
Og	King of Bashan whose bed was thirteen feet long and six feet wide	Deuteronomy 3:11
Ishbi-Benob	Abishai killed this giant, who toted a spear whose tip weighed in excess of seven pounds	2 Samuel 21:16
An unnamed giant	This giant from Philistia who had twelve toes and twelve fingers was killed by David's nephew	1 Chronicles 20:6

❄ TEN OLD TESTAMENT TEXTS REFERRED ❄
TO IN THE NEW TESTAMENT

Book	Reference
Jonah	Matthew 12:39
Genesis	Mark 10:8
Numbers	John 3:14
Isaiah	Luke 4:18
Deuteronomy	Luke 10:27
Joel	Acts 2:17
Habakkuk	Romans 1:17
Zechariah	Matthew 21:5
Daniel	Mark 13:14
Psalms	Matthew 27:46

❄ MORE HYMNS FROM SCRIPTURE ❄

Philippians 2:5–11

> And being found in appearance as a man,
>> he humbled himself
>>> and became obedient to death—
>>>> even death on a cross! (v. 8)

Revelation 4:8, 11

> Holy, holy, holy
>> is the Lord God Almighty,
> who was, and is, and is to come.
>> . . . You are worthy, our Lord and God,
>>> to receive glory and honor and power,
> for you created all things,
>> and by your will they were created
>> and have their being.

Revelation 5:9–10, 12–13

> Worthy is the Lamb, who was slain,
>> to receive power and wealth and wisdom and strength
>> and honor and glory and praise!
> . . . To him who sits on the throne and to the Lamb
> be praise and honor and glory and power,
> for ever and ever! (vv. 12–13)

❧ POSTURES OF PRAYER ❧

Lying prostrate (Deut. 9:18) • Sitting (1 Kings 19:4) • Bowing (Ps. 95:6) •
Standing (Mark 11:25) • Kneeling (Eph. 3:14) • Lifting hands (1 Tim. 2:8)

❧ SOLOMON'S WORDS FOR THOSE TEMPTED ❧
BY AN ADULTEROUS PERSON

My son, pay attention to my wisdom,
    listen well to my words of insight,
that you may maintain discretion
    and your lips may preserve knowledge.
For the lips of an adulteress drip honey,
    and her speech is smoother than oil;
but in the end she is bitter as gall,
    sharp as a double-edged sword.
Her feet go down to death;
    her steps lead straight to the grave.
She gives no thought to the way of life;
    her paths are crooked, but she knows it not.
Now then, my sons, listen to me;
    do not turn aside from what I say.
Keep to a path far from her,
    do not go near the door of her house,
lest you give your best strength to others
    and your years to one who is cruel,
lest strangers feast on your wealth
    and your toil enrich another man's house.
At the end of your life you will groan,
    when your flesh and body are spent.
. . . Why be captivated, my son, by an adulteress?
    Why embrace the bosom of another man's wife?
For a man's ways are in full view of the LORD,
    and he examines all his paths.
The evil deeds of a wicked man ensnare him;
    the cords of his sin hold him fast.
He will die for lack of discipline,
    led astray by his own great folly.

—Proverbs 5:1–11, 20–23

❧ THE JUDGMENT OF GOD ❧

Here are accounts of some of the most severe judgments of God:

■ On the appointed day Herod, wearing his royal robes, sat on his throne and delivered a public address to the people. They shouted, "This is the voice of a god, not of a man." Immediately, because Herod did not give praise to God, an angel of the Lord struck him down, and he was eaten by worms and died. (Acts 12:21–23)

■ But when his [Nebuchadnezzar] heart became arrogant and hardened with pride, he was deposed from his royal throne and stripped of his glory. He was driven away from people and given the mind of an animal; he lived with the wild donkeys and ate grass like cattle; and his body was drenched with the dew of heaven, until he acknowledged that the Most High God is sovereign over the kingdoms of men and sets over them anyone he wishes. (Dan. 5:20–21)

■ When they came to the threshing floor of Nacon, Uzzah reached out and took hold of the ark of God, because the oxen stumbled. The LORD's anger burned against Uzzah because of his irreverent act; therefore God struck him down and he died there beside the ark of God. (2 Sam. 6:6–7)

■ Now the people complained about their hardships in the hearing of the LORD, and when he heard them his anger was aroused. Then fire from the LORD burned among them and consumed some of the outskirts of the camp. (Num. 11:1)

■ But while the meat was still between their teeth and before it could be consumed, the anger of the LORD burned against the people, and he struck them with a severe plague. (Num. 11:33)

■ Then Peter said, "Ananias, how is it that Satan has so filled your heart that you have lied to the Holy Spirit and have kept for yourself some of the money you received for the land? Didn't it belong to you before it was sold? And after it was sold, wasn't the money at your disposal? What made you think of doing such a thing? You have not lied to men but to God." When Ananias heard this, he fell down and died. And great fear seized all who heard what had happened. Then the young men came forward, wrapped up his body, and carried him out and buried him. (Acts 5:3–6).

❆ MEMORABLE FORTY-DAY PERIODS IN SCRIPTURE ❆

The number forty appears often enough in Scripture to catch our attention. The number almost always measures periods of suffering or hardship. In the days before watches and the widespread use of calendars, a complete lunar cycle, which is longer than a month, served as a handy indicator of a long time. Consider:

- For Noah, forty days of rain provided a godly prophet with proof that God does what he says he will do.
- For Moses, forty days on Mount Sinai taught him to approach the Holy One without distraction in order to hear God speak and have time to reflect on his Word.
- For the twelve spies, forty days in the Promised Land gave them a chance to see firsthand just why it was called "a land flowing with milk and honey."
- For David the shepherd, forty days of listening to Goliath's blasphemy against Israel's God were enough to convince him that with God's help he could do what others were too timid to do: destroy the Philistine giant.
- For Elijah, forty days were proof that God was more than adequate to care for his physical needs before the prophet faced a series of difficult challenges.
- For Jonah, forty days revealed to him that God not only had the power to get a prophet to a place he didn't want to go, but he could change the hearts of the pagan Ninevites, who didn't want anything to do with him.
- For Jesus, forty days in the wilderness were a necessary period of spiritual basic training where he needed to stand up to evil before he moved to the front lines of public ministry.
- For the disciples, forty days served as their five and a half weeks of purposeful preparation. It was a kind of on-the-job-training following Jesus's resurrection.

❆ THE NOT-SO-NICE KINGS OF ISRAEL ❆

King	Description	Reference
Jeroboam	Perverted the worship of God	1 Kings 11–14
Ahab	Wicked husband of Jezebel	1 Kings 16–22
Ahaziah	Wicked son of Ahab	1 Kings 22–2 Kings 1
Menahem	A brutal king	2 Kings 15
Ahaz	Sacrificed his son to a pagan god	2 Kings 16
Jehoiakim	Persecuted Jeremiah and burned his prophetic scroll	2 Kings 23–24; Jeremiah 36
Jehoiachin	Incurred the wrath of God for his ungodly actions	2 Kings 24

❊ NON-ISRAELITE KINGS OF THE BIBLE ❊

Name	Nationality	References
Agag	Amalekite	1 Samuel 15:8–9
Nahash	Ammonite	1 Samuel 11:1–11
Hanun	Ammonite	2 Samuel 10:1–4
Baalis	Ammonite	Jeremiah 40:14
Tiglath-Pileser III	Assyrian	2 Kings 15:29; 16:7, 10
Shalmaneser V	Assyrian	2 Kings 17:3–6; 18:9–11
Sargon II	Assyrian	Isaiah 20
Merodach-Baladan	Babylonian	2 Kings 20:12; Isaiah 39:1
Evil-Merodach	Babylonian	2 Kings 25:27–28
Bera	Canaanite	Genesis 14:2–24
Adoni-Zedek	Canaanite	Joshua 10:1–27
Jabin	Canaanite	Joshua 11:1–11
Shishak	Egyptian	1 Kings 14:25–26
Neco	Egyptian	2 Kings 23:29–30
Hophra	Egyptian	Jeremiah 44:30; 46:1–26
Balak	Moabite	Numbers 22–24
Eglon	Moabite	Judges 3:12–22
Mesha	Moabite	2 Kings 3:4–27
Artaxerxes	Persian	Ezra 7:1; Nehemiah 2:1
Achish	Philistine	1 Samuel 21:10–14
Ben-Hadad I	Syrian	1 Kings 20:1–34
Ben-Hadad II	Syrian	2 Kings 5:5–6
Hazael	Syrian	1 Kings 19:15; 2 Kings 8:7–15, 28–29
Rezin	Syrian	2 Kings 16:5–9
Hiram	Tyrian	1 Kings 5

❋ OLD TESTAMENT JUDGES AND ❋
WHAT THEY ACCOMPLISHED

The ancient Hebrew judges served as living representatives of God's justice and judgments. They seldom spoke for God (like prophets) but acted on God's behalf as charismatic leaders during troubled periods. They appeared on the scene when God's people repented over national sinfulness and called out for divine intervention. Note their varied careers and levels of effectiveness:

Judge	Accomplishment	Reference
Othniel	Captured a Canaanite city	Judges 1:12–13
Ehud	Killed the king of Moab and conquered the Moabites	Judges 3:12–30
Shamgar	Killed six hundred Philistines with an oxgoad (wooden rod)	Judges 3:31
Deborah	Convinced Barak to take on Sisera and his troops	Judges 4
Gideon	Defeated 120,000 Midianites with an army of three hundred	Judges 6–8
Tola	Maintained Israel's freedom from surrounding nations for twenty-three years	Judges 10:1–2
Jair	Delivered thirty Israelite cities from their enemies	Judges 10:3–5
Jephthah	Made a vow and then defeated the Ammonites	Judges 10:6–12:7
Ibzan	Maintained Israel's freedom from surrounding nations for seven years	Judges 12:8–10
Elon	Maintained Israel's freedom from surrounding nations for ten years	Judges 12:11–12
Abdon	Maintained Israel's freedom from surrounding nations for eight years	Judges 12:13–15
Samson	Killed one thousand Philistines with the jawbone of a donkey and demolished a pagan temple as he died	Judges 13–16

❈ GREAT BALLS OF FIRE ❈

- There the angel of the LORD appeared to him in flames of fire from within a bush. Moses saw that though the bush was on fire it did not burn up. (Exod. 3:2)
- By day the LORD went ahead of them in a pillar of cloud to guide them on their way and by night in a pillar of fire to give them light, so that they could travel by day or night. (Exod. 13:21)
- Mount Sinai was covered with smoke, because the LORD descended on it in fire. The smoke billowed up like smoke from a furnace; the whole mountain trembled violently. (Exod. 19:18)
- To the Israelites the glory of the LORD looked like a consuming fire on top of the mountain. (Exod.24:17)
- On the day the tabernacle, the Tent of the Testimony, was set up, the cloud covered it. From evening till morning the cloud above the tabernacle looked like fire. (Num. 9:15)
- Now the people complained about their hardships in the hearing of the LORD, and when he heard them his anger was aroused. Then fire from the LORD burned among them and consumed some of the outskirts of the camp. (Num. 11:1)
- And fire came out from the LORD and consumed the 250 men who were offering the incense. (Num. 16:35)
- With the tip of the staff that was in his hand, the angel of the LORD touched the meat and the unleavened bread. Fire flared from the rock, consuming the meat and the bread. And the angel of the LORD disappeared. (Judg. 6:21)
- Then the fire of the LORD fell and burned up the sacrifice, the wood, the stones and the soil, and also licked up the water in the trench. (1 Kings 18:38)
- By the same word the present heavens and earth are reserved for fire, being kept for the day of judgment and destruction of ungodly men. (2 Pet. 3:7)

❈ NAMES OF SATAN ❈

Have you ever wondered why people don't shout out the devil's name when they hit their thumbs with a hammer? God is the expletive of choice. Even if you never took French in high school, you probably can figure out that the word *devil* is nothing more than the contraction of two words that indicate the evil one (*D'evil*). That is how Scripture portrays the devil: he is the personification of evil. In addition to the devil, he is called Satan (Job 1:6) and Lucifer (Isa. 14:12 KJV). Using animal metaphors, the Bible likens him to a serpent (Gen. 3) and a roaring lion (1 Pet. 5:8). Using human terms, he is called the father of lies (John 8:44).

❄ THE SEVEN CHURCHES IN REVELATION ❄

Church	Commendation	Criticism	Reference
Ephesus	Good deeds, hard work, perseverance, doctrinal purity	Lost their first love	Revelation 2:1–7
Smyrna	Rich in the things that matter in spite of afflictions and poverty	Prone to fear future suffering	Revelation 2:8–11
Pergamum	Faithfulness in the midst of evil	Embraced heretical teaching	Revelation 2:12–17
Thyatira	Exhibited love, faith, service, and perseverance	Accommodated sexual immorality and false teaching	Revelation 2:18–29
Sardis		Appeared to be spiritually alive but were dead	Revelation 3:1–6
Philadelphia	Had kept Christ's Word in spite of having little strength		Revelation 3:7–13
Laodicea		Were lukewarm in spiritual passion and unaware of their spiritual nakedness	Revelation 3:14–22

❄ THE OCCUPATIONS OF THOSE CALLED TO PREACH ❄

- Isaiah was a writer (2 Chron. 26:22).
- Jeremiah was a priest (Jer. 1:1).
- Ezekiel was a priest (Ezek. 1:3).
- Amos was a shepherd (Amos 1).
- Peter was a fisherman (Luke 5:3–4).
- Paul was a bounty hunter and a tentmaker (Acts 9; 18:3).

❧ FAMOUS WATERING HOLES IN THE OLD TESTAMENT ❧

- The well called Beer Lahai Roi where God got Hagar's attention (Gen. 16:14)
- The well in the Paran wilderness where God encountered Hagar again (Gen. 21:19)
- The well in Beersheba where Abraham and Abimelech made a covenant (Gen. 21:30)
- The well in Nahor where Abraham's servant discovered Rebekah (Gen. 24)
- The wells Isaac reopened in the Valley of Gerar (Gen. 26:18)
- The well in Paddan Aram where Jacob first met Rachel (Gen. 29)
- The well in Midian where Moses first encountered Zipporah (Exod. 2)
- The spring of Marah where God provided the Israelites fresh water (Exod. 15:22–25)
- The well in Elim where God supplied water for his people en route to Mount Sinai (Exod. 15:27)
- The spring of Rephidim where God provided water for his people in the desert (Exod. 17)
- The well the Israelites dug in the desert (Num. 21)
- The Bahurim well where David's spies hid from Absalom (2 Sam. 17:18)
- The well in Ramah where Saul searched for David (1 Sam. 19:22)
- The Sirah well where Abner and Joab met (2 Sam. 3:26)
- The well in Bethlehem that was the source of homesickness for David (2 Sam. 23:15)
- Jacob's well in Samaria where Jesus engaged a woman in conversation about her spiritual thirst (John 4:6)

❧ FAMOUS LAST WORDS ❧

"I have sinned by betraying innocent blood."—Judas (Matt. 27:4 NASB)

"Let me die with the Philistines!" —Samson (Judg. 16:30 NASB)

"Lord, do not hold this sin against them."—Stephen (Acts 7:60)

"It is finished!"—Jesus (John 19:30)

"Draw your sword and thrust me through with it, otherwise these uncircumcised will come and abuse me." —Saul (1 Chron. 10:4 NASB)

"Behold, thou hast driven me out this day from the ground; and from thy face I shall be hidden; and I shall be a fugitive and a wanderer on the earth, and whoever finds me will slay me." —Cain (Gen. 4:14 RSV)

❀ FAMINES ❀

Famine	Circumstances	Reference
In Canaan	Caused Abraham to go to Egypt	Genesis 12:10
In Canaan	Caused Isaac to go to Philistia	Genesis 26:1
In Canaan	Caused Jacob's eleven sons to go to Egypt	Genesis 41:54–57
In Canaan	Caused Naomi and her husband to move to Moab	Ruth 1:1
In Judah	Caused by Saul's ungodliness	2 Samuel 21:1
In Israel	Caused by the sins of Ahab and Israel	1 Kings 17:1
In Gilgal	Where Elisha remedied the poison in the stew pot	2 Kings 4:38–41
In Samaria	Where four lepers were instrumental in the salvation of a city	2 Kings 6:25; 7
In Israel	Where it was proved beyond a doubt that there was still a prophet of God in Israel	2 Kings 8:1–6
In Jerusalem	Caused by Nebuchadnezzar's siege	2 Kings 25:2–3
In Jerusalem	Which resulted in a response to God and revival among the people	Nehemiah 5:1–13
Throughout the Roman Empire	Predicted by the prophet Agabus	Acts 11:28

❀ THE EMOTIONS OF JESUS ❀

Emotion	How Demonstrated	Reference
Grief	Jesus wept when he learned Lazarus had died.	John 11:35
Deep sorrow	Jesus "began to be sorrowful and troubled" in the Garden of Gethsemane.	Matthew 26:37
Joy	Jesus prayed with joy to his Father after hearing the report of the seventy-two disciples' mission trip.	Luke 10:21
Love	Jesus felt love for the rich young ruler who couldn't give up his wealth to follow Jesus.	Mark 10:21
Empathy	Jesus, while dying on the cross, asked John to care for his mother.	John 19:26
Anger	Jesus made a whip and drove the moneychangers out of God's temple.	John 2:13–17

❋ MOUNTAINS OF NOTE ❋

Mountains	Location	Significance	Reference
Ararat	Turkey	Where Noah's ark landed	Genesis 8:4
Moriah	Jerusalem	Where Abraham offered up Isaac; where Solomon built his temple	Genesis 22:2; 2 Chronicles 3:1
Gilead	Jordan	Where Jacob and Laban made their covenant	Genesis 31:20–49
Horeb	A chain of mountains in the Sinai Peninsula	Where Moses encountered the burning bush	Exodus 3:1
Sinai	The highest peak of the Horeb range	Where Moses received the Ten Commandments	Exodus 20
Hor	Near Kadesh and the border of Edom	Where Aaron died and was buried	Numbers 20:23–28
Pisgah (Nebo)	East of the Dead Sea	Where Moses viewed the Promised Land	Deuteronomy 3:27
Gerizim	In Samaria between Judah and Galilee	Where the blessings of obedience were to be proclaimed	Deuteronomy 27:12–13
Pisgah	East of the Dead Sea	Where Moses died and was buried	Deuteronomy 34:1, 5–6
Gilboa	South of the Plain of Esdraelon	Where King Saul killed himself	1 Samuel 31:1–6
Carmel	West of the Sea of Galilee, overlooking the Mediterranean Sea	Where Elijah challenged the prophets of Baal	1 Kings 18:19
Hermon	Near Caesarea Philippi	Where Jesus was transfigured	Matthew 17:1–2
Olives	Across the Kidron Valley from Jerusalem	Where Jesus wept over Jerusalem	Luke 19:37, 41
Mars Hill	Next to the marketplace in Athens	Where Paul addressed the Athenians	Acts 17:16–22 (KJV)

❈ THE BENEFITS OF EACH BEATITUDE ❈

Beatitude	Benefit	Reference
Blessed are the poor in spirit.	Theirs is the kingdom of heaven.	Matthew 5:3
Blessed are those who mourn.	They will be comforted.	Matthew 5:4
Blessed are the meek.	They will inherit the earth.	Matthew 5:5
Blessed are those who hunger and thirst for righteousness.	They will be filled.	Matthew 5:6
Blessed are the merciful.	They will be shown mercy.	Matthew 5:7
Blessed are the pure in heart.	They will see God.	Matthew 5:8
Blessed are the peacemakers.	They will be called sons of God.	Matthew 5:9
Blessed are those who are persecuted because of righteousness.	Theirs is the kingdom of heaven.	Matthew 5:10
Blessed are you when people insult you, persecute you and falsely say all kinds of evil against you because of me.	Great is your reward.	Matthew 5:11

❈ THE INCREDIBLE SUFFERINGS OF JOB ❈

- His oxen and donkeys were stolen (Job 1:14–15).
- His servants and livestock were killed (Job 1:16).
- His camels were stolen (Job 1:17).
- More of his servants were killed (Job 1:17).
- His sons and daughters were killed (Job 1:18–19).
- He was covered with boils (Job 2:7).
- His wife grumbled at him (Job 2:9).
- His three friends falsely accused him of doing wrong (Job 4–37).

❄ DEAD MEN WALKING ❄

- During the days when Saul was King of Israel, he consulted a medium in Endor. The witch claimed to see a spirit coming up from out of the ground. As she described what she saw, Saul knew it must be the prophet Samuel who had died (1 Sam. 28:13–14).

- When Lazarus died, he was wrapped in grave clothes and buried in a cave. At the sound of Jesus's voice commanding him to "come out," the mummy walked out of the tomb to the amazement of those who stood around (John 11:43–44).

- Following his death and resurrection, Jesus went to Hades and preached to the spirits in prison who had disobeyed God (1 Pet. 3:19).

- After his resurrection, Jesus suddenly appeared on the road that connects Jerusalem with Emmaus and began walking with two disciples. Initially they didn't recognize him, but later they realized they'd been walking and talking with someone who had been dead but wasn't anymore (Luke 24:31).

- After the encounter with Jesus on the road to Emmaus, the two disciples returned to Jerusalem. They found the other disciples gathered in a large room. Suddenly Jesus appeared in their midst without having entered through the door. All who were present thought he was a ghost, but he showed them his wounds and pointed out his flesh and bones. He then sat and ate with them to dispel their assertion that he was a dead man walking (Luke 24:36–43).

❄ NOT-SO-VIRTUOUS WOMEN OF THE BIBLE ❄

Tamar . . . . Disguised herself as a prostitute so she could sleep with her father-in-law (Gen. 38:13–18)

Athaliah . . . . Destroyed the whole royal family of the house of Judah (2 Chron. 22:10)

Delilah . . . . Manipulated and betrayed Samson (Judg. 16:4–22)

Medium of Endor . . Called Samuel's spirit up from the ground to speak with Saul (1 Sam. 28:7–25)

Herodias . . . . Wife of Herod who demanded that John the Baptist's head be cut off (Mark 6:14–28)

Sapphira . . . . Kept money back from the apostles (Acts 5:1–11)

❦ DREAMS JOSEPH INTERPRETED ❦

The patriarch Jacob's son Joseph was a dreamer. He also demonstrated unusual skill and confidence in interpreting dreams. This ability got him into trouble as a youth but got him out of trouble as an adult. Joseph understood that dreams and their meanings could come from God. Note the following:

Who had the dream?	What was the dream about?	What did it mean?	Where can I read about it?
Joseph	Joseph's brothers' bundles of grain bowed down to his bundle.	Joseph would someday rule over his brothers.	Genesis 37:5–8
Joseph	The sun, moon, and stars were bowing down to Joseph.	Joseph would someday rule over his brothers.	Genesis 37:9–10
Pharaoh's chief cupbearer	The cupbearer made wine and gave it to Pharaoh.	The cupbearer would be removed from jail and serve Pharaoh again.	Genesis 40:9–13
Pharaoh's chief baker	Birds ate the food that the baker was bringing to Pharaoh.	Pharaoh was going to hang the baker and cut off his head.	Genesis 40:16–19
Pharaoh	Seven plump cows were drinking when seven skinny and ugly cows came and ate them.	Egypt would have seven years with plenty of food followed by seven years of famine.	Genesis 41:17–21, 25–31
Pharaoh	Seven good ears of corn grew but were swallowed up by seven withered and bad ears of corn.	Egypt would have seven years with plenty of food followed by seven years of famine.	Genesis 41:22–32

❈ MIRACLES RELATED TO FOOD ❈

Miraculous Food	Setting	Reference
Manna	When the Israelites complained in the wilderness about not having food, God provided white flakes that tasted like wafers of honey. They appeared supernaturally each morning with the dew.	Exodus 16
Quail	When the Israelites complained about not having meat in the wilderness, God sent quail.	Numbers 11
Never-ending bread	When the widow of Zarephath was preparing to cook one last meal for herself and her son (convinced they would starve to death after that), Elijah the prophet commanded her to mix what little flour and oil she had left and bake it into bread. As a result of her obedience, the flour and oil miraculously never ran out for three years.	1 Kings 17
Stew	At Elisha's command, his servant prepared a pot of stew. A stranger put poisonous vines and gourds in it. The prophet added flour to supernaturally neutralize the poison.	2 Kings 4
Barley loaves	During a famine in Gilgal, someone brought Elisha twenty barley loaves. He insisted that it be distributed to a crowd of one hundred fellow prophets. The bread was miraculously multiplied so that all were fed. There was even bread left over.	2 Kings 4
Wine	At a wedding reception in the village of Cana, the host ran out of wine. Jesus asked that jugs be filled with water, and he supernaturally turned it into a vintage that was the talk of the party.	John 2

❋ MIRACLES RELATED TO FOOD—CONT. ❋

Miraculous Food	Setting	Reference
Five barley loaves and two fish	When a crowd of several thousand gathered to hear Jesus preach, a boy donated his lunch. Jesus multiplied the small quantity of bread and fish to feed everyone—with extra to spare.	John 6
Bread	As two disciples were slowly walking from Jerusalem to their home in Emmaus, they met a man who inquired why they seemed so sad. They told him of Jesus's crucifixion. When they invited the stranger into their home, they recognized he was the risen Christ as he broke the bread before them and then miraculously disappeared.	Luke 24
Broiled fish	Following the Crucifixion, Jesus appeared to his disciples. Although he had a resurrected body that could penetrate walls, he could still eat. Jesus asked for food and they gave him fish.	Luke 24
Fish and bread	Sometime after the Resurrection, Jesus stood on the beach cooking fish and bread while the disciples labored in vain on the Sea of Galilee to catch fish. Jesus called out to them to cast their nets on the other side of the boat, and they caught 153 fish. Later they ate on the beach.	John 21

❋ TWO-TIMERS, THREE-TIMERS, AND MORE ❋

The following men had more than one wife:

Lamech • Jacob • Esau • Gideon • Elkanah • David •
Solomon* • Ashhur • Shaharaim • Rehoboam • Abijah • Joash

* Solomon had seven hundred wives.

❋ THE TRUMPETS ❋

Trumpets serve as attention-getters. Whether in their ancient form as animal horns or in their various developments in metal, trumpets provide the context of arrivals, announcements, and in Scripture, God's pronouncements. The book of Revelation describes seven trumpet fanfares that will accompany devastating judgments on the world. Consider:

Trumpet	*The Ensuing Judgment*	*Reference*
The First Trumpet	A third of the earth, a third of the trees, and all of the grass are burned up.	Revelation 8:7
The Second Trumpet	A third of the sea turns to blood, a third of the creatures in the sea die, and a third of the ships are destroyed.	Revelation 8:8–9
The Third Trumpet	A third of the waters turn bitter, and many people die.	Revelation 8:10–11
The Fourth Trumpet	A third of the day, a third of the night, and a third of the stars are darkened.	Revelation 8:12
The Fifth Trumpet	An abyss is opened, out of which come locusts with tails like those of scorpions. For five months they torture those who do not have the seal of God on their heads.	Revelation 9:1–11
The Sixth Trumpet	Four angels and two hundred million horses and riders are released to kill a third of mankind.	Revelation 9:13–19
The Seventh Trumpet	Many scholars believe this trumpet refers to the second coming of Jesus—when he returns to conquer his enemies.	Revelation 11:15–19

❄ THE TWELVE MYTHS OF CHRISTMAS ❄

A number of details have slipped into popular conceptions of the Christmas story that aren't actually in the Bible. The story of Jesus's birth can be found in Matthew 2 and Luke 2.

1. Mary rode a donkey to Bethlehem.

2. An innkeeper refused Mary and Joseph entry into his inn.

3. Mary gave birth to Jesus the very night they reached Bethlehem.

4. Jesus was born in December.

5. Jesus was born in a stable or a cave.

6. Jesus was surrounded by animals at his birth.

7. The baby Jesus didn't cry.

8. The angels sang when they appeared to the shepherds.

9. The angels told the shepherds to follow the star.

10. The wise men were kings (there were three of them), and they traveled by camel.

11. The wise men visited Jesus at the stable.

12. Herod's edict to slaughter male infants was to be enforced nationwide.

❄ GONE TO THE DOGS ❄

Dogs didn't have the highest reputation in biblical times. To be thought of as a dog was an insult (1 Sam. 17:43; 24:14), and calling oneself a dog was a way of showing humility before someone in authority (2 Sam. 9:8; 2 Kings 8:13). Dogs ate the bodies of the dead, the most shameful fate a person could contemplate (1 Kings 21:23–26). The Bible also compares evildoers to dogs (Ps. 22:16; Rev. 22:15). Nevertheless, dogs were used to guard sheep (Job 30:1), and people kept them as pets (Matt. 15:26–27).

❦ PROPHETS AND THEIR MESSAGES ❦

The Old Testament prophets delivered God's words to the world. They frequently addressed people with "This is what God says [Thus sayeth the Lord]." Some of them wrote, and all of their messages were recorded. But they were God's living representatives, often expressing God's directives, displeasure, and judgment. They announced God's future actions. As has often been said, the prophets were fore-tellers and forthtellers. They are listed below chronologically:

Name	Place and Time	Message
Obadiah	Judah, ca. 853 BC	For mistreating God's people, Edom will be judged.
Joel	Judah, ca. 835–796 BC	Repent before judgment comes that is worse than a mere plague of locusts.
Jonah	Israel, Assyria, 793–753 BC	Assyria will be judged unless it repents.
Amos	Israel, 760–750 BC	Work toward social justice, and aid the poor.
Hosea	Israel, 752–715 BC	Israel has sinned and will be judged.
Micah	Judah, 742–687 BC	Both Israel and Judah will be punished, but this is to show God's love for them.
Isaiah	Judah, 740–681 BC	Judgment is coming, but afterward Judah will be restored.
Zephaniah	Judah, 640–621 BC	God will judge all nations but will show mercy to the faithful.
Nahum	Judah, 663–612 BC	Assyria will be judged for oppressing God's people.
Jeremiah	Judah, 627–586 BC	Repentance will delay judgment. Faithfulness will bring hope.
Habakkuk	Judah, 612–589 BC	Despite the prosperity of the wicked, God is just and will destroy evil.
Daniel	Babylon, 605–536 BC	All of history is in God's hands.
Ezekiel	Babylon, 593–571 BC	Judah was destroyed because of its sins, but God will restore the faithful.
Haggai	Judah, ca. 520 BC	Finish rebuilding the temple.
Zechariah	Judah, ca. 520 BC	Finish the temple. A future king will establish an eternal kingdom.
Malachi	Judah, ca. 430 BC	Judah will be punished for its sin, but the repentant will be blessed.

❋ NUMBERS OF NOTE ❋

The six days of creation.

The forty days of the Flood.

The four hundred years of Egyptian captivity.

The three days Jonah spent in the belly of the fish.

The seventy years of captivity in Babylon.

The forty days of Jesus's temptation in the wilderness.

The three days Jesus was in the grave.

The four Gospels.

The number of the Beast is 666.

The sixty-six books of the Bible.

The three persons of the Godhead.

The twelve disciples of Jesus.

The seventy-two disciples Jesus sent out.

The 153 fish the disciples caught following Jesus's resurrection.

The nine fruits of the Spirit.

The Ten Commandments.

The nine Beatitudes.

Five loaves and two fish.

David picked up five smooth stones.

The twelve tribes of Israel.

The twelve spies.

The thirty-nine stripes of Jesus's flogging.

Jesus's encounter with the chief priests at the age of twelve.

The thousand-year millennial reign

The Three Taverns in Rome.

The animals taken into the ark two by two.

Eighteen people killed when the Tower of Siloam fell on them.

A crippled man waited at the pool for thirty-eight years.

A woman hemorrhaged for twelve years.

The two witnesses during the Tribulation.

The 144,000 who will be saved as mentioned in Revelation.

The thirty pieces of silver.

Forgiving seventy times seven times.

❋ JAILBIRDS ❋

You might be surprised to know that the following Bible figures spent time behind bars:

Joseph (Gen. 39) • The baker (Gen. 40) • The cupbearer (Gen. 40) • Simeon (Gen. 42:24) • Samson (Judg. 16:21) • Hoshea (2 Kings 17:4) • Hanani (2 Chron. 16:10) • Jeremiah (Jer. 38:6) • Zedekiah (Jer. 39:7) • Daniel (Dan. 6:16–17) • John the Baptist (Matt. 14:3) • Barabbas (Matt. 27:16) • James (Acts 12:1–2) • Peter (Acts 12:4) • Paul (Acts 16:23) • Silas (Acts 16:23) • John exiled on Patmos (Rev. 1:9)

❧ CONFIRMED PROPHETIC OCCURRENCES ❧

Prophecy	References	Fulfillment
The city of Tyre will be destroyed and never rebuilt.	Ezekiel 26:3–21	Attacked by Nebuchadnezzar, Alexander the Great, Antigonus, and the Muslims. The original city is mostly underwater.
The city of Samaria will be destroyed.	Hosea 13:16; Micah 1:6	Attacked by Sargon, Alexander the Great, and John Hyrcanus.
The city of Ashkelon will be devastated.	Zephaniah 2:4–7	Ashkelon was devastated by Sulton Bibars in AD 1270.
The kingdom of Ammon will be invaded by people from the east.	Ezekiel 25:3–4	Emir Abdullah invaded Ammon and built his palaces there.
The kingdom of Edom will be destroyed.	Isaiah 34:6–15; Jeremiah 49:17–18; Ezekiel 25:13–14; 35:5–7	The Israelites killed eighteen thousand Edomites.
The city of Nineveh will be overtaken by a flood.	Nahum 1:8–10; 2:6; 3:10–19	A flood weakened Nineveh's defenses, allowing enemies to come in and destroy the city.
The city of Babylon will become desolate and ruined.	Isaiah 13:19–22; 14:23; Jeremiah 51:26, 43	Cyrus invaded and took the city of Babylon. After the invasion the city slowly began to decay.

❧ FAMOUS WEDDINGS ❧

Isaiah married Rebekah (Gen. 24). • Jacob married Leah and Rachel (Gen. 29). • Joseph married Asenath (Gen. 41). • David married Bathsheba (2 Sam. 11). • Solomon married seven hundred women (1 Kings 11). • Hosea married Gomer (Hosea 1). • Joseph married Mary (Matt. 1). • Jesus turned water into wine at a wedding in Cana (John 2).

❈ A RELATIVE ISSUE ❈

Cain was rivals with his brother, Abel (Gen. 4).

Adam and Eve's third son was Seth (Gen. 4).

Sarah was Abraham's half sister (Gen. 20:12).

Lot was Abraham's nephew (Gen. 12:5).

Jacob was rivals with his brother, Esau (Gen. 27).

Joseph had eleven brothers (Gen. 37).

Jethro was Moses's father-in-law (Exod. 18).

Aaron was Moses's brother (Exod. 4).

Miriam was Moses's sister (Num. 26:59).

Naomi was Ruth's mother-in-law (Ruth 1).

Ruth was King David's great-grandmother (Ruth 4).

King David cared for Mephibosheth, Jonathan's son (2 Sam. 9).

Esther was Mordecai's cousin (Esther 2).

Mary was the mother of Jesus and his brothers (Matt. 12).

Andrew and Peter were brothers (Matt. 4:18).

James and John were brothers (Matt. 4:21).

James and John's mother made a special request of Jesus (Matt. 20).

Peter's mother-in-law was healed by Jesus (Mark 1).

Mary and Martha were sisters (Luke 10).

Lazarus was the brother of Mary and Martha (John 11).

John Mark was Barnabas's cousin (Col. 4:10).

Paul's unidentified nephew saved his life (Acts 23).

Andronicus and Junias were Paul's relatives in prison with him (Rom. 16).

Lois was Timothy's grandmother (2 Tim. 1).

Eunice was Timothy's mother (2 Tim. 1).

❈ GODLY SONS OF GODLESS FATHERS ❈

Godly Son	Godless Father
Jonathan	Saul
Asa	Abijah
Joash	Ahaziah
Hezekiah	Ahaz
Josiah	Amon

❊ THE STRONGEST MAN EVER TO LIVE ❊

The Spirit of God gave Samson incredible strength. The following verses give a small sampling of his power:

- As they approached the vineyards of Timnah, suddenly a young lion came roaring toward him. The Spirit of the LORD came upon him in power so that he tore the lion apart with his bare hands as he might have torn a young goat. (Judg. 14:5–6)
- Then the Spirit of the LORD came upon him in power. He went down to Ashkelon, struck down thirty of their men, stripped them of their belongings and gave their clothes to those who had explained the riddle. Burning with anger, he went up to his father's house. (Judg. 14:19)
- As he approached Lehi, the Philistines came toward him shouting. The Spirit of the LORD came upon him in power. The ropes on his arms became like charred flax, and the bindings dropped from his hands. Finding a fresh jawbone of a donkey, he grabbed it and struck down a thousand men. (Judg. 15:14–15)
- But Samson lay there only until the middle of the night. Then he got up and took hold of the doors of the city gate, together with the two posts, and tore them loose, bar and all. He lifted them to his shoulders and carried them to the top of the hill that faces Hebron. (Judg. 16:3)

❊ LONGEST NAMES OF BIBLICAL ❊
PEOPLES AND LOCATIONS

Name	Reference	Definition
Abel-beth-maachah	1 Kings 15:20 (KJV)	A city in Israel.
Almon-diblathaim	Numbers 33:46–47 (KJV)	A settlement of the Israelites.
Apharsathchites	Ezra 4:9 (KJV)	The inhabitants of a city. were called by this name.
Helkath-hazzurim	2 Samuel 2:16 (KJV)	A battlefield in Gibeon.
Ramathaim-zophim	1 Samuel 1:1 (KJV)	The town where Samuel was born.
Bashan-havoth-jair	Deuteronomy 3:14 (KJV)	The name given to the country of Argob by Jair.
Chephar-haammonai	Joshua 18:24 (KJV)	An Israelite city.
Kibroth-hattaavah	Deuteronomy 9:22 (KJV)	The Jews wandered through this location in the desert.
Sela-hammahlekoth	1 Samuel 23:28 (KJV)	Where Saul attacked the Philistines.

❊ BEAUTIFUL PEOPLE OF THE BIBLE ❊

Name	Description	Reference
Sarai	"I know what a beautiful woman you are."	Genesis 12:11
Rebekah	"The girl was very beautiful."	Genesis 24:16
Rachel	"Rachel was lovely in form, and beautiful."	Genesis 29:17
Joseph	"Now Joseph was well-built and handsome."	Genesis 39:6
David	"He was only a boy, ruddy and handsome."	1 Samuel 17:42
Abigail	"She was a woman of good understanding, and of a beautiful countenance."	1 Samuel 25:3 (KJV)
Bathsheba	"The woman was very beautiful."	2 Samuel 11:2
Tamar	"The beautiful sister of Absalom son of David."	2 Samuel 13:1
Absalom	"There was not a man so highly praised for his handsome appearance."	2 Samuel 14:25
Adonijah	"He was also very handsome."	1 Kings 1:6
Solomon's wife	"How beautiful, you are, my darling!" [says Solomon].	Song of Songs 1:15
Solomon	"My lover is radiant and ruddy" [says Solomon's wife].	Song of Songs 5:10
Assyrian warriors	"All of them handsome young men."	Ezekiel 23:6
Hebrew exiles	"Young men without any physical defect, handsome."	Daniel 1:4

❊ TOWN DRUNKS ❊

Noah (Gen. 9:21) • Lot (Gen. 19:33) • Nabal (1 Sam. 25:36) •
Elah (1 Kings 16:9) • Uriah (2 Sam. 11:13) • Amnon (2 Sam. 13:28) • Guests
of King Xerxes (Esther 1:8) • Belshazzar (Dan. 5:4–5) • Some Christians
in the Corinthian church (1 Cor. 11:21)

❋ TEARS THROUGH THE YEARS ❋

- Hagar cried for Ishmael (Gen. 21:16).
- Abraham cried for Sarah at her funeral (Gen. 23:2).
- Jacob cried tears of joy when he found Rachel (Gen. 29:11).
- Esau and Jacob both cried when they reunited after many years (Gen. 33:4).
- Jacob cried when his sons led him to believe that Joseph had been killed (Gen. 37:35).
- Joseph cried when he was reunited with his brothers (Gen. 45:14–15).
- The Egyptians cried when they discovered their firstborn children were dead (Exod. 12:30).
- The Israelites cried because they craved meat (Num. 11:4).
- The Israelites cried when Moses died (Deut. 34:8).
- Samson's wife cried trying to get a favor (Judg. 14:16).
- Naomi cried as she left Moab en route for Bethlehem (Ruth 1:9).
- Hannah cried because she couldn't have children (1 Sam. 1:10).
- Saul cried when he regretted opposing David (1 Sam. 24:16).
- The Israelites cried upon learning of Samuel's death (1 Sam. 25:1).
- The Jewish captives cried when they were captives in Babylon (Ps. 137:1).
- Esther cried as she pleaded for her people (Esther 8:3).
- Nehemiah cried over the broken-down walls of Jerusalem (Neh. 1:4).
- Jeremiah wept because God's people had been killed and exiled and their city had been destroyed (Lam. 3:48–51).
- An unidentified woman anointed Jesus's feet with her tears (Luke 7:38).
- Jesus cried over Jerusalem (Luke 19:41).
- Mary cried over Lazarus (John 11:33).
- The elders in Ephesus cried as they hugged Paul good-bye (Acts 20:37).

❋ SHORTEST AND LONGEST NAMES IN THE BIBLE ❋

Shortest	Longest
Eve	Maher-Shalal-Hash-Baz
Ur	Mephibosheth
Ai	Nebuchadnezzar
Hur	Chushan-Rishathaim
Er	Hazarmaveth
Nun	Tiglath-Pileser
Dan	Zaphenath-Paneah

✸ THE "ONE ANOTHER" VERSES OF THE BIBLE ✸

Accept one another . . . . Romans 15:7

Admonish one another . . . . Colossians 3:16

Bear one another's burdens . . . . Galatians 6:2 (KJV)

Bear with one another . . . . Ephesians 4:2

Build up one another . . . . Romans 14:19

Care for one another . . . . 1 Corinthians 12:25 (KJV)

Comfort one another . . . . 1 Thessalonians 4:18 (KJV)

Confess faults to one another . . . . James 5:16 (KJV)

Be devoted to one another . . . . Romans 12:10

Encourage one another . . . . 1 Thessalonians 5:11

Forgive one another . . . . Ephesians 4:32

Greet one another . . . . Romans 16:16

Be honest with one another . . . . Colossians 3:9

Honor one another . . . . Romans 12:10

Be hospitable to one another . . . . 1 Peter 4:9

Be kind to one another . . . . Ephesians 4:32

Love one another . . . . Romans 13:8

Pray for one another . . . . James 5:16

Be of the same mind
with one another . . . . Romans 15:5

Serve one another . . . . Galatians 5:13

Spur one another on . . . . Hebrews 10:24

Submit to one another . . . . Ephesians 5:21

✸ THE MIRACLES OF THE APOSTLE PAUL ✸

- Caused Elymas to go blind (Acts 13).
- Healed a crippled man (Acts 14).
- Laying on of hands resulted in speaking in tongues and prophecy (Acts 19).
- Handkerchiefs and aprons that touched Paul became a means of healing (Acts 19).
- Raised Eutychus from the dead (Acts 20).
- Did not die from a snakebite (Acts 28).
- Healed Publius's father of high fever and dysentery (Acts 28).
- Healed many sick on the island of Malta (Acts 28).

❈ SERMONS OF SIGNIFICANCE ❈

Who Preached It	Title	Theme	Text
Jonah	Nineveh Sermon	Get right with God.	Jonah 3:4
John the Baptist	Ramblings	Repent.	Matthew 3:7–12
Jesus	Sermon on the Mount	Values of God's kingdom.	Matthew 5:1–7:27
Jesus	Sermon on the Plain	Values of God's kingdom.	Luke 6:17–49
Jesus	Olivet Discourse	End-times expectations.	Matthew 24–25; Mark 13; Luke 21:5–36
Peter	Pentecost Explained	Accept Jesus as Messiah.	Acts 2:14–39
Peter	Speaking of Healing	Believe on the risen Christ.	Acts 3:12–26
Stephen	My Defense	Judgment of Israel's hard heart.	Acts 7:1
Peter	God Has No Favorites	The gospel is not just for Jews.	Acts 10:34–43
Paul	Old Testament History 101	God's promises have come to pass.	Acts 13:16–41
Paul	Mars Hill Meditation	The unknown God has a name.	Acts 17:22–31
Paul	My Testimony	God has called me.	Acts 22:1–21
Paul	A Defense Before Felix	Hope in the Resurrection.	Acts 24:10–21
Paul	A Defense Before Agrippa	Become a Christian like me.	Acts 26:2–29

❈ ROMAN OFFICIALS NAMED IN THE BIBLE ❈

Theophilus, an unidentified official (Luke 1) • Caesar Augustus, an emperor (Luke 2) • Pilate, a governor (Matt. 27) • Cornelius, a centurion (Acts 10) • Sergius Paulus, a proconsul (Acts 13) • Gallio, a proconsul (Acts 18) • Claudius Lysias, a chief captain (Acts 23) • Felix, a governor (Acts 24) • Festus, a governor (Acts 25) • Julius, a centurion (Acts 27) • Erastus, a city official (Rom. 16)

✺ WHAT THE BIBLE SAYS ABOUT NATURE ✺

- What God created is good (Gen. 1).
- Nature provides a picture of godly and ungodly living (Ps. 1).
- Nature will eventually pass away, but God's Word and people live on forever (Isa. 40).
- Nature and creation point to the greatness of God (Ps. 8).
- The heavens above us provide a rationale for God's existence (Ps. 19).
- The beauty of creation is a picture of praise to God (Ps. 98).
- God's care for nature is indicative of his concern for our welfare (Matt. 6).
- God's qualities and divine nature are observable in the natural order (Rom. 1).
- The creation anticipates the coming of the kingdom of God in its fullness (Rom. 8).

✺ THE FUTURE OF NATURE ✺

Here are a few Bible passages that shed light on the changes that nature will go through upon the return of Christ:

- "The wolf and the lamb will feed together, / and the lion will eat straw like the ox, / but dust will be the serpent's food / They will neither harm nor destroy / on all my holy mountain," says the LORD. (Isa. 65:25)

- The creation waits in eager expectation for the sons of God to be revealed. For the creation was subjected to frustration, not by its own choice, but by the will of the one who subjected it, in hope that the creation itself will be liberated from its bondage to decay and brought into the glorious freedom of the children of God. We know that the whole creation has been groaning as in the pains of childbirth right up to the present time. (Rom. 8:19–22)

- The wolf will live with the lamb, / the leopard will lie down with the goat, / the calf and the lion and the yearling together; / and a little child will lead them. / The cow will feed with the bear, / their young will lie down together, / and the lion will eat straw like the ox. / The infant will play near the hole of the cobra, / and the young child put his hand into the viper's nest. / They will neither harm nor destroy / on all my holy mountain, / for the earth will be full of the knowledge of the LORD / as the waters cover the sea. (Isa. 11:6–9)

- You will go out in joy / and be led forth in peace; / the mountains and hills / will burst into song before you, / and all the trees of the field / will clap their hands. (Isa. 55:12)

❊ SUICIDES ❊

Person	Circumstances	Reference
Abimelech	Had his armor bearer kill him after being wounded by a woman	Judges 9:54
Samson	Intentionally caused a building to collapse on top of himself	Judges 16:30
Saul	Fell on his sword after losing a battle to the Philistines	1 Samuel 31:4
Saul's servant	Followed his master's lead	1 Samuel 31:5
Ahithophel	Hanged himself after Absalom rejected his advice	2 Samuel 17:23
Zimri	Set the palace ablaze while inside so as not to be captured as a prisoner	1 Kings 16:18
Judas Iscariot	Hanged himself after feeling remorse over betraying Jesus	Matthew 27:5

❊ SMALL OBJECTS WITH A BIG LESSON ❊

Splinters. Toothaches. Ingrown toenails. Small discomforts can radically impact our lives. Jesus didn't talk about such things, even though he probably struggled with them (especially the splinters in his father's carpentry shop). But the Bible does illustrate how little things pack a wallop.

For example, Jesus said that just a tiny amount of faith (the size of a mustard seed) can move mountains (Matt. 17:20). He took a little boy's lunch of five small barley loaves and two fish and multiplied it supernaturally to feed a crowd of thousands (John 6:41). Jesus warned about getting all excited about the speck of sawdust in another's eye without making the effort to remove the plank in your own (Matt. 7:3). He got angry at the Pharisees for their selective obedience and accused them of straining out a gnat and swallowing a camel (Matt. 23:24).

But Jesus also said that God the Father is aware of the tiniest of things. He sees sparrows when they fall (Matt. 10:29), and he knows the number of hairs on a person's head (Matt. 10:30). When Jesus saw the widow drop two small coins in the temple treasury, he said such sacrificial giving was far more generous than that of most (Luke 21:2–3). Even the apostle Paul saw big lessons in little things. He made the observation that sin was like yeast, in that it expands exponentially (1 Cor. 5:6).

❧ DREAMS AND VISIONS IN THE OLD TESTAMENT ❧

Jacob . . . . When he reached a certain place, he stopped for the night because the sun had set. Taking one of the stones there, he put it under his head and lay down to sleep. He had a dream in which he saw a stairway resting on the earth, with its top reaching to heaven, and the angels of God were ascending and descending on it. (Gen. 28:11–12)

Joseph . . . . Joseph had a dream, and when he told it to his brothers, they hated him all the more. He said to them, "Listen to this dream I had: We were binding sheaves of grain out in the field when suddenly my sheaf rose and stood upright, while your sheaves gathered around mine and bowed down to it." His brothers said to him, "Do you intend to reign over us? Will you actually rule us?" And they hated him all the more because of his dream and what he had said. (Gen. 37:5–8)

Pharaoh . . . . When two full years had passed, Pharaoh had a dream: He was standing by the Nile, when out of the river there came up seven cows, sleek and fat, and they grazed among the reeds. After them, seven other cows, ugly and gaunt, came up out of the Nile and stood beside those on the riverbank. And the cows that were ugly and gaunt ate up the seven sleek, fat cows. Then Pharaoh woke up. (Gen. 41:1–5)

Nebuchadnezzar . . . . I, Nebuchadnezzar, was at home in my palace, contented and prosperous. I had a dream that made me afraid. As I was lying in my bed, the images and visions that passed through my mind terrified me. So I commanded that all the wise men of Babylon be brought before me to interpret the dream for me. (Dan. 4:4–6)

Daniel . . . . In the first year of Belshazzar king of Babylon, Daniel had a dream, and visions passed through his mind as he was lying on his bed. He wrote down the substance of his dream. (Dan. 7:1)

❈ WHY DO CHRISTIANS EXPERIENCE PAIN? ❈

To develop their perseverance

Consider it pure joy, my brothers, whenever you face trials of many kinds, because you know that the testing of your faith develops perseverance. Perseverance must finish its work so that you may be mature and complete, not lacking anything. (James 1:2–4)

Because God is disciplining them for their good

Endure hardship as discipline; God is treating you as sons. For what son is not disciplined by his father? (Heb. 12:7)

To increase their fellowship with Christ

I want to know Christ and the power of his resurrection and the fellowship of sharing in his sufferings, becoming like him in his death. (Phil. 3:10)

As a result of the Fall

When the woman saw that the fruit of the tree was good for food and pleasing to the eye, and also desirable for gaining wisdom, she took some and ate it. She also gave some to her husband, who was with her, and he ate it.

> . . . To the woman he said, / "I will greatly increase your pains in childbearing; / with pain you will give birth to children. / Your desire will be for your husband, / and he will rule over you."

> To Adam he said, "Because you listened to your wife and ate from the tree about which I commanded you, 'You must not eat of it,' / Cursed is the ground because of you; / through painful toil you will eat of it / all the days of your life. / It will produce thorns and thistles for you, / and you will eat the plants of the field. / By the sweat of your brow / you will eat your food / until you return to the ground, / since from it you were taken; / for dust you are / and to dust you will return." (Gen. 3:6, 16–19)

To promote obedience

It was good for me to be afflicted / so that I might learn your decrees. (Ps. 119:71)

To provide opportunity to patiently endure

But how is it to your credit if you receive a beating for doing wrong and endure it? But if you suffer for doing good and you endure it, this is commendable before God. (1 Pet. 2:20)

To humble and test them

Remember how the LORD your God led you all the way in the desert these forty years, to humble you and to test you in order to know what was in your heart, whether or not you would keep his commands. (Deut. 8:2)

As a result of sin

Sin entered the world through one man, and death through sin, and in this way death came to all men, because all sinned. (Rom. 5:12)

❄ FEMININE HEROES ❄

Rahab was a prostitute in Jericho. But when she met the two Israelites spying out the city they were about to capture, she offered them hospitality and risked her life to hide them and help them escape (Josh. 2).

Deborah was the only woman among Israel's premonarch judges. She united the young nation and led a successful battle against Sisera and his Canaanite army (Judg. 4–5).

Jael became a hero when she enticed Sisera, commander of Canaan's army, into her tent. She hammered a tent peg through his head while he slept (Judg. 4).

Ruth was the Moabite woman who left her homeland and family and traveled to Bethlehem with her widowed mother-in-law, Naomi. Once in Israel, Ruth, a young widow herself, met and married Boaz and won the hearts of those who met her. She became the great-grandmother of Israel's greatest king, David (Ruth 1–4).

Abigail was the wife of a wealthy sheepherder (Nabal) who insulted David. She proved herself a hero by thinking quickly and acting resourcefully to shower David and his soldiers with food and hospitality. Her behavior kept the Israel's would-be king from seeking revenge. When Nabal died, David married her (1 Sam. 25).

Mary, the mother of Jesus, was declared a hero by her cousin even before the unmarried teenage girl gave birth to the Savior. It was Elizabeth who announced, "Blessed are you among women." Enduring the hurtful barbs of those who misjudged her son's miraculous conception, she lived with the knowledge of his mysterious identity and stood at the foot of his cross as he died (Luke 1).

❉ THE MYSTERIOUS ANGEL OF THE LORD ❉

The angel of the Lord appears numerous times throughout the Bible. Many scholars believe this angel is a manifestation of the preincarnate Christ.

- The angel of the LORD found Hagar near a spring in the desert; it was the spring that is beside the road to Shur. And he said, "Hagar, servant of Sarai, where have you come from, and where are you going?" "I'm running away from my mistress Sarai," she answered. Then the angel of the LORD told her, "Go back to your mistress and submit to her." The angel added, "I will so increase your descendants that they will be too numerous to count." (Gen. 16:7–10)

- God heard the boy crying, and the angel of God called to Hagar from heaven and said to her, "What is the matter, Hagar? Do not be afraid; God has heard the boy crying as he lies there. Lift the boy up and take him by the hand, for I will make him into a great nation." (Gen. 21:17–18)

- But the angel of the LORD called out to him from heaven, "Abraham! Abraham!" "Here I am," he replied. "Do not lay a hand on the boy," he said. "'Do not do anything to him. Now I know that you fear God, because you have not withheld from me your son, your only son." (Gen. 22:11–12)

- There the angel of the LORD appeared to him in flames of fire from within a bush. Moses saw that though the bush was on fire it did not burn up. (Exod. 3:2)

- The angel of the LORD went up from Gilgal to Bokim and said, "I brought you up out of Egypt and led you into the land that I swore to give to your forefathers. I said, 'I will never break my covenant with you, and you shall not make a covenant with the people of this land, but you shall break down their altars.' Yet you have disobeyed me. Why have you done this?" (Judg. 2:1–2)

- "Curse Meroz," said the angel of the LORD. / "Curse its people bitterly, / because they did not come to help the LORD, / to help the LORD against the mighty." (Judg. 5:23)

- The angel of the LORD came and sat down under the oak in Ophrah that belonged to Joash the Abiezrite, where his son Gideon was threshing wheat in a winepress to keep it from the Midianites. When the angel of the LORD appeared to Gideon, he said, "The LORD is with you, mighty warrior." (Judg. 6:11–12)

- As the flame blazed up from the altar toward heaven, the angel of the LORD ascended in the flame. Seeing this, Manoah and his wife fell with their faces to the ground. When the angel of the LORD did not show himself again to Manoah and his wife, Manoah realized that it was the angel of the LORD. "We are doomed to die!" he said to his wife. "We have seen God!" (Judg. 13:20–22)

- When the angel stretched out his hand to destroy Jerusalem, the LORD was grieved because of the calamity and said to the angel who was afflicting the people, "Enough! Withdraw your hand." The angel of the LORD was then at the threshing floor of Araunah the Jebusite. (2 Sam. 24:16)

- Then the angel of the LORD said, "LORD Almighty, how long will you withhold mercy from Jerusalem and from the towns of Judah, which you have been angry with these seventy years?" (Zech. 1:12)

- On that day the LORD will shield those who live in Jerusalem, so that the feeblest among them will be like David, and the house of David will be like God, like the Angel of the LORD going before them. (Zech. 12:8)

❈ DEMON POSSESSION ❈

"The devil made me do it!" wasn't just a lame excuse in Bible days. For many unfortunate individuals, that was the reason they writhed in convulsive fits on the ground, practiced self-destructive behavior, or viciously attacked others with supernatural strength. The unseen presence of evil entered both children and adults and controlled their actions and physical abilities. Often this demonic possession resulted in a person's inability to speak, to see, or to stand up straight.

When Jesus wasn't healing the sick, he was delivering some poor soul from the demons that held them hostage. Matthew described Jesus's determination to exorcize demons who dehumanized those he loved:

Jesus went throughout Galilee, teaching in their synagogues, preaching the good news of the kingdom, and healing every disease and sickness among the people. News about him spread all over Syria, and people brought to him all who were ill with various diseases, those suffering severe pain, the demon-possessed, those having seizures, and the paralyzed, and he healed them. (Matt. 4:23–24)

❀ DAVID VERSUS SAUL ❀

Why is David known as the "good king," and Saul as the "bad king"? Both kings sinned greatly against God. Saul distrusted God and performed a sacrifice he shouldn't have, and he also disobeyed God by not entirely destroying the Amalekites. But David also committed very serious sins (i.e., adultery and murder). Many believe that the reason David is known as the "good king" is because he genuinely repented when confronted with his sin. Because of this, God forgave him and continued to bless him. The following psalm gives a picture of David's repentant heart.

A Psalm of David
When the Prophet Nathan Came to Him
After David Had Committed Adultery with Bathsheba

Have mercy on me, O God,
according to your unfailing love;
according to your great compassion
blot out my transgressions.
Wash away all my iniquity
and cleanse me from my sin.

For I know my transgressions,
and my sin is always before me.
Against you, you only, have I sinned
and done what is evil in your sight,
so that you are proved right when you speak
and justified when you judge.

. . . Create in me a pure heart, O God,
and renew a steadfast spirit within me.
Do not cast me from your presence
or take your Holy Spirit from me.
Restore to me the joy of your salvation
and grant me a willing spirit, to sustain me
—Psalm 51:1–4, 10–12

❀ JOHNS OF THE BIBLE ❀

Jonathan, the son of Saul (1 Sam. 13:16) • John the Baptist (Matt. 3) •
John, the son of Zebedee (Matt. 4) • John, the father of Simon and Andrew
(John 21:16) • John Mark, the cousin of Barnabas (Acts 12:12)

❦ IMPORTANT AND NOT-SO-IMPORTANT DIMENSIONS ❦

- **Noah's Ark:** 450 feet long, 75 feet wide, and 45 feet high

- **The Tabernacle:** Outer fence: 150 feet long and 75 feet wide.

- **The Holy Place:** 30 feet long and 15 feet wide

- **The Ark of the Covenant:** 3.75 feet long, 2.25 feet wide, 2.25 feet high

- **Solomon's Temple:** 90 feet long, 30 feet wide, 45 feet high

- **The Holy of Holies:** 30 feet long, 30 feet wide, and 30 feet high

- **The New Jerusalem (the heavenly city):** 1,400 miles long, 1,400 miles wide, and 1,400 miles high

❦ SCIENTIFIC ACCURACIES IN THE BIBLE ❦

Accuracy	*Reference*
The earth is spherical.	Isaiah 40:22
The earth is suspended.	Job 26:7
Mountains and canyons exist in the sea.	2 Samuel 22:16
Springs and fountains exist in the sea	Genesis 7:11; 8:2; Proverbs 8:28
The existence of ocean currents	Psalm 8:8
The hydrologic cycle	Job 26:8; 36:27–28; Psalm 135:7
Facts about the human bloodstream	Leviticus 17:11
The second law of thermodynamics (Energy in our universe is slowly used up and eventually none will be left. This law allows us to conclude that the universe will eventually degenerate.)	Psalm 102:25–26; Romans 8:18–23; Hebrews 1:10–12

❧ A BAKER'S DOZEN ❧

Ever wonder how bread figures into the Old and New Testaments?

1. Bread was such a basic item that the word *bread* in the Bible often simply means "food."

2. Bread was usually made of barley (Judg. 7:13) or wheat (Exod. 29:2).

3. Bread typically took the form of thin wafers or loaves (1 Chron. 23:29), which were often used to scoop food from a common bowl (Matt. 26:23).

4. People saw bread as the gift of God (Ps. 104:14–15).

5. Pharaoh had his chief baker executed (Gen. 40:20–22).

6. During Passover the Israelites were to eat bread made without yeast to symbolize the haste with which they left Egypt (Exod. 12:39; Deut. 16:3).

7. In the wilderness God gave the Israelites a bread called "manna" (Exod. 16:14–15).

8. Ravens served Elijah bread and meat (1 Kings 17:6).

9. Satan tempted Jesus to turn stones into bread when he was hungry in the desert (Matt. 4:3).

10. On two separate occasions Jesus miraculously increased the supply of bread to feed a whole crowd with plenty left over (John 6:1–13; Mark 8:1–8).

11. Jesus called himself the Bread of Life (John 6:35).

12. Jesus told the disciples not to take bread with them when he sent them out to preach (Mark 6:8). This left them free to receive the hospitality of the towns they were visiting.

13. Jesus gave bread a new significance at the Last Supper. There he turned it into a symbol of his body, which he was about to sacrifice for the salvation of the world (Luke 22:19).

❈ PROPHECIES FULFILLED BY JESUS ❈

▨ He was born of a woman (Gen. 3:15; Gal. 4:4).

▨ He was a descendant of Abraham (Gen. 12:3; Rom. 9:5).

▨ He was a descendant of the tribe of Judah (Gen. 49:10; Heb. 7:14).

▨ He was a descendant of King David (2 Sam. 7:12; Luke 1:32).

▨ He was born of a virgin (Isa. 7:14; Matt. 1:20–23).

▨ He was called Immanuel (Isa. 7:14; Matt. 1:23).

▨ He was born in Bethlehem (Mic. 5:2; Matt. 2:1).

▨ He was declared the Son of God (Ps. 2:7; Matt. 3:17)

▨ He obscured the truth from unbelievers (Isa. 6:9–10; Matt. 13:10).

▨ He was rejected (Isa. 53:3; John 1:11).

▨ He made a triumphal entry into Jerusalem (Zech. 9:9; Matt. 21:1–11).

▨ His friend betrayed him for thirty pieces of silver (Ps. 41:9; Matt. 26:14–16, 47–50).

▨ He was a man of sorrows (Isa. 53:3; Matt. 26:37).

▨ His feet and hands were pierced (Ps. 22:16; John 20:24–28).

▨ Some gambled for his clothes (Ps. 22:18; Luke 23:34).

▨ His bones were not broken (Exod. 12:46; John 19:33–36).

▨ He was buried in a rich man's grave (Isa. 53:9; Matt. 27:57–60).

▨ He rose from the dead (Ps. 16:10; Matt. 28:1–6).

- The Nephilim were on the earth in those days—and also afterward—when the sons of God went to the daughters of men and had children by them. They were the heroes of old, men of renown. (Gen. 6:4)

- Just as it is written: "Jacob I loved, but Esau I hated." (Rom. 9:13)

- If anyone comes to me and does not hate his father and mother, his wife and children, his brothers and sisters—yes, even his own life—he cannot be my disciple. (Luke 14:26)

- If they want to inquire about something, they should ask their own husbands at home; for it is disgraceful for a woman to speak in the church. (1 Cor. 14:35)

- Do you not know that the wicked will not inherit the kingdom of God? Do not be deceived: Neither the sexually immoral nor idolaters nor adulterers nor male prostitutes nor homosexual offenders nor thieves nor the greedy nor drunkards nor slanderers nor swindlers will inherit the kingdom of God. (1 Cor. 6:9–10)

- Wives, submit to your husbands, as is fitting in the Lord. (Col. 3:18)

- What if God, choosing to show his wrath and make his power known, bore with great patience the objects of his wrath—prepared for destruction? (Rom. 9:22)

❀ WAS EVE CUTE? ❀

God created the world and proclaimed that it was good. God told Adam that he must not eat of a certain tree: "But you must not eat from the tree of the knowledge of good and evil, for when you eat of it you will surely die" (Gen. 2:17). Adam and Eve sinned against God by eating from this tree, causing life on earth to become very different. Not only were the innocence and moral purity of their souls shattered, but death, decay, disease, and all other forms of imperfection entered the physical world. Before their sin, there was no bad breath, oily skin, or any other physical imperfection. Following this train of thought allows us to assume that before the Fall, Adam and Eve were without any defect—spiritually or physically. So yes, Eve was cute.

❦ OLD TESTAMENT MIRACLES ❦

Miracle	Reference
Creation	Genesis 1
The birth of Isaac	Genesis 17:17; 18:12; 21:2
Moses's staff becomes a serpent	Exodus 4:2–3
The parting of the Red Sea	Exodus 14:22
Manna for the Israelites	Exodus 16
A shout tumbles the walls of Jericho	Joshua 6:20
The sun stands still	Joshua 10:12–14
Elijah raises the widow's son from death	1 Kings 17:17–24
Fire sent on Elijah's sacrifice	1 Kings 18:38
Fire consumes the captains and their men	2 Kings 1:10–12
The parting of the Jordan River	2 Kings 2:8
Elijah taken up into heaven	2 Kings 2:11
Elisha multiplies twenty loaves of bread to feed one hundred men	2 Kings 4:42–22
The Arameans scared into a panic by the sound of a supernatural army	2 Kings 7:6–7
Dead man comes to life after he's thrown on Elisha's bones	2 Kings 13:21
Three men stand in a furnace and are not harmed	Daniel 3:23–27
Daniel is thrown into a lions' den and is unharmed	Daniel 6:21–23

❦ FOREIGN NATIONS MENTIONED IN THE BIBLE ❦

Assyria (2 Chron. 33:11) • Babylon (Dan. 4:30) • Ethiopia
(Acts 8:27) • Egypt (Gen. 37:28) • Greece (John 12:20) •
Persia (Dan. 6:15) • Spain (Rom. 15:28)

❊ TOOLS USED TO MAKE DECISIONS ❊

People in the Bible used a number of methods for discerning God's will and affirming God's call when they didn't trust their own judgment.

Miraculous Signs
- Abraham's servant and Rebekah at the well (Gen. 24)
- Moses's hand and staff (Exod. 4:1–7)
- Gideon's fleece (Judg. 6:36–40)
- Hezekiah and the moving shadow (2 Kings 20:1–11)

Lots
- The distribution of the land to each of Israel's tribes (Num. 26:55)
- Finding the guilty party in the storm at sea (Jon. 1:7)
- Deciding the owner of Jesus's clothes (Matt. 27:35)
- Finding a new apostle to replace Judas (Acts 1:26)

The Urim and Thummim
- We're not sure what these were—probably stones—but the priest in Israel used them to determine God's decisions (Exod. 28:30; Lev. 8:8; Num. 27:21; Deut. 33:8; 1 Sam. 28:6; Ezra 2:63; Neh. 7:65).

Dreams
- Pharaoh (Gen. 41:1–36)
- Joseph of Nazareth (Matt. 1:18–25)
- The Magi (Matt. 2:12)
- Paul (Acts 16:9–10)

Prophets
- Saul and the donkeys (1 Sam. 9:3–10)
- The man of God and the old prophet (1 Kings 13:11–34)
- Jeroboam's son (1 Kings 14:1–16)
- Ahab's battle (1 Kings 20:13–14)
- Micaiah and the king of Israel (1 Kings 22:1–28)

Mediums
- Saul consulted a medium to find out the outcome of his battle with the Philistines, even though God had forbidden the Israelites to do this (1 Sam. 28).

❈ SECONDS OF THE BIBLE ❈

▪ Second oldest book in the Old Testament: **Genesis** ⋆

▪ Second longest book of the Bible: **Isaiah**

▪ Second shortest book of the Bible: **2 John**

▪ Second oldest man to ever live: **Jared** (962 years)

▪ Second sin committed in the Bible: **murder**

▪ The second miracle of Jesus: "That evening after sunset the people brought to Jesus all the sick and demon-possessed. The whole town gathered at the door, and Jesus healed many who had various diseases. He also drove out many demons, but he would not let the demons speak because they knew who he was" **(Mark 1:32–34).**

▪ The second person of the triune Godhead: **Jesus**

▪ Second sinner in the Bible: **Adam** (he ate the forbidden fruit)

▪ The second murderer of the Bible: **Lamech**

▪ The second person to be created: **Eve**

▪ The second-to-last verse of the Bible: "He who testifies to these things says, 'Yes, I am coming soon.' Amen. Come, Lord Jesus" **(Rev. 22:20).**

⋆According to most scholars.

❈ HOW MANY TIMES IS GOD ❈ MENTIONED IN THE BIBLE?

New International Version: 3,442 verses

New American Standard Bible: 3,441 verses

The Message: 3,635 verses

King James Version: 3,561 verses

❄ BAD EVENTS THAT RESULTED IN GOOD ❄

Bad Events	Good Result	Reference
Joseph is sold into slavery by his brothers and ends up in Egypt.	Joseph becomes second in command to Pharaoh.	Genesis 37
Ruth is left as a lonely widow.	She marries Boaz and becomes part of the messianic line.	Ruth 1–4
David commits adultery with Bathsheba.	The couple become parents of Solomon, the wisest man who ever lived.	2 Samuel 12:24; 1 Kings 4:29–34
Jesus is crucified.	Jesus's sacrificial death on the cross assuages God's wrath for mankind.	John 19; Romans 5:1–11
After he rises from the dead, Jesus leaves his disciples and returns to heaven.	Jesus sends his Holy Spirit to empower his followers.	Acts 1; John 14
Stephen is stoned by the religious leaders in Jerusalem, and the fearful followers of Christ scatter.	The gospel spreads throughout the Roman Empire.	Acts 7–8
Paul's prayer that God remove a thorn in his flesh is not answered the way he wishes.	Paul experiences God's grace—which enables him to live with the problem.	2 Corinthians 12

❈ PARABLES ABOUT SEEDS AND WEEDS ❈

Name	Reference	Meaning
The Parable of the Sower	Matthew 13:1–9, 18–23; Mark 4:1–9, 13–20	A Christian who hears and understands the Word will produce the fruit of the Spirit.
The Parable of the Weeds	Matthew 13:24–30, 36–43	Christians and non-Christians will be together until Christ returns to separate them.
The Parable of the Growing Seed	Mark 4:26–29	The faith of a Christian will grow by the power of God.
The Parable of the Mustard Seed	Mark 4:30–32	Although a Christian's faith and spiritual vitality start off small, they will eventually become great.

❈ OLD TESTAMENT PROPHECIES OF JESUS'S BIRTH ❈

Prophecy	Old Testament Reference	New Testament Fulfillment
The Messiah would come from the tribe of Judah.	Genesis 49:10	Luke 3:33
A young woman would give birth to a baby and name him Immanuel.	Isaiah 7:14	Matthew 1:22–23
A child would be born who would be known as Wonderful Counselor, Mighty God, Everlasting Father, and the Prince of Peace.	Isaiah 9:6	John 1:14
The Messiah would be born in Bethlehem.	Micah 5:2	Luke 2:4

Adam, when asked why he ate the fruit, said, "The woman you put here with me—she gave me some fruit from the tree, and I ate it" (Gen. 3:12).

Eve, when asked why *she* ate the fruit, said, "The serpent deceived me, and I ate" (Gen. 3:13).

Cain, when asked where his murdered brother was, said, "I don't know. . . . Am I my brother's keeper?" (Gen. 4:9).

Lot, when told to flee from Sodom to the mountains, said, "But I can't flee to the mountains; this disaster will overtake me, and I'll die" (Gen. 19:19).

Jacob said to his brother, Esau, just before heading to an entirely different location, "My lord knows that the children are tender and that I must care for the ewes and cows that are nursing their young. If they are driven hard just one day, all the animals will die. So let my lord go on ahead of his servant, while I move along slowly at the pace of the droves before me and that of the children, until I come to my lord in Seir" (Gen. 33:13–14).

Moses, when told to free the Israelites, said, "Who am I, that I should go to Pharaoh and bring the Israelites out of Egypt? . . . What if they do not believe me or listen to me and say, 'The LORD did not appear to you'? . . . O Lord, I have never been eloquent, neither in the past nor since you have spoken to your

servant. I am slow of speech and tongue" (Exod. 3:11; 4:1, 10).

Aaron, when asked about the golden calf, said, "Do not be angry, my lord. . . . You know how prone these people are to evil. They said to me, 'Make us gods who will go before us. As for this fellow Moses who brought us up out of Egypt, we don't know what has happened to him.' So I told them, 'Whoever has any gold jewelry, take it off.' Then they gave me the gold, and I threw it into the fire, and out came this calf!" (Exod. 32:22–24).

Ten of Israel's spies, after scouting out the Promised Land, said, "We can't attack those people; they are stronger than we are. . . . The land we explored devours those living in it. All the people we saw there are of great size. We saw the Nephilim there (the descendants of Anak come from the Nephilim). We seemed like grasshoppers in our own eyes, and we looked the same to them" (Num. 13:31–33).

Saul, when asked why he illegally made a sacrifice, said, "When I saw that the men were scattering, and that you did not come at the set time, and that the Philistines were assembling at Micmash, I thought, 'Now the Philistines will come down against me at Gilgal, and I have not sought the LORD's favor.' So I felt compelled to offer the burnt offering" (1 Sam. 13:11–12).

Saul, when asked why he disregarded God's instructions to destroy everything in a battle, said, "But I did obey the LORD. . . . I went on the mission the LORD assigned me. I completely destroyed the Amalekites and brought back Agag their king. The soldiers took sheep and cattle from the plunder, the best of what was devoted to God, in order to sacrifice them to the LORD your God at Gilgal" (1 Sam. 15:20–21).

Elijah, when asked why he was hiding in a cave, said, "I have been very zealous for the LORD God Almighty. The Israelites have rejected your covenant, broken down your altars, and put your prophets to death with the sword. I am the only one left, and now they are trying to kill me too" (1 Kings 19:10).

Guests, when invited to a banquet, said: "I have just bought a field, and I must go and see it. Please excuse me." "I have just bought five yoke of oxen, and I'm on my way to try them out. Please excuse me." "I just got married, so I can't come" (Luke 14:18–20).

The unfaithful servant, when asked why he saved rather than investing, said, "Master . . . I knew that you are a hard man, harvesting where you have not sown and gathering where you have not scattered seed. So I was afraid and went out and hid your talent in the ground. See, here is what belongs to you" (Matt. 25:24–25).

Felix, after hearing Paul preach about righteousness, self-control, and the coming judgment, said fearfully, "That's enough for now! You may leave. When I find it convenient, I will send for you" (Acts 24:25).

❦ SNAKES AND SERPENTS ❦

- Satan, in the form of a serpent, tempted Adam and Eve to eat fruit from the tree of the knowledge of good and evil. (Genesis 3:1–4, 14–15)

- Aaron's staff became a serpent. (Exodus 7:9)

- Moses made a bronze snake and put it up on a pole. Anyone who was bitten by a poisonous snake would look at the bronze snake and be cured. (Numbers 21:8–9)

- Paul was bitten by a poisonous viper and was not harmed. (Acts 28:3–5)

- Satan is referred to as an "ancient serpent." The serpent will be seized by an angel and will be bound for 1,000 years. (Revelation 20:2)

❧ THE BEATITUDES IN THE BOOK OF REVELATION ❧

We are used to thinking of the Beatitudes as the list of blessings Jesus pronounced at the beginning of the Sermon on the Mount. But the book of Revelation pronounces its own set of blessings.

- Blessed are those who read the words of Revelation's prophecy and obey them (see Rev. 1:3; 22:7).

- Blessed are believers who die, for they will rest and receive the reward for their good deeds (see Rev. 14:13).

- Blessed are those who watch for Jesus's return and keep their spiritual clothes wrapped around them, for they will not be caught naked when he appears (see Rev. 16:15).

- Blessed are those who are invited to the marriage supper of the Lamb (see Rev. 19:9).

- Blessed are those who participate in the first resurrection; the second death will not affect them, and they will be priests and will reign with Christ for a thousand years (see Rev. 20:6).

- Blessed are those who are cleansed and forgiven by the blood of Jesus, for they will be able to enter the gates of the New Jerusalem and to eat from the tree of life (see Rev. 22:14).

❧ DELECTABLE MEALS ❧

Dish	*Enjoyed by*
Dust	The serpent (Gen. 3:14)
Gold-flaked water	The Israelites (Exod. 32:20)
Hopping insects	The Israelites (Lev. 11:22); John the Baptist (Mark 1:6)
Honey from lion's carcass	Samson and his family (Judg. 14:8–9)
Grass	Nebuchadnezzar (Dan. 4:33; 5:21)

✢ MEN WHO HEARD VOICES ✢

- Adam heard God ask about Adam's whereabouts (Gen. 3:9).

- Noah heard God's warning about the Flood (Gen. 6:13).

- Abraham heard God's promise to make him the father of many nations (Gen. 12:1–3).

- Jacob heard God repeat the promise he made to Jacob's father, Abraham (Gen. 28:13–15).

- Moses heard God speak from a burning bush to tell him to lead the Israelites out of Egypt (Exod. 3:1–10).

- Joshua heard God tell him to cross the Jordan River and to lead the Israelites into the Promised Land (Josh. 1:1–5).

- Samuel as a young boy heard God announce his judgment against the high priest's family (1 Sam. 3:1–14).

- Elijah heard God tell him to get back to work (1 Kings 19:9–18).

- Isaiah and Ezekiel each heard God call him to take God's message to the people of Israel (Isa. 6; Ezek. 2).

- Jeremiah heard God call him to be a prophet to the people of Judah (Jer. 1).

- At his baptism, Jesus heard a voice from heaven declaring him to be God's beloved Son (Mark 1:9–11). Peter, James, and John later heard the same voice delivering the same message about Jesus when he was transfigured in front of them (Matt. 17:5–6).

- Paul (named Saul at the time) heard the voice of Jesus asking why Paul was persecuting him (Acts 9:1–4).

- Peter heard God declaring Gentiles clean (Acts 10).

- John heard Jesus revealing the future of the world (Rev. 1:9–19).

❊ THE TEN LONGEST BOOKS IN THE BIBLE ❊

Book	Length
Psalms	150 chapters
Isaiah	66 chapters
Jeremiah	52 chapters
Genesis	50 chapters
Ezekiel	48 chapters
Job	42 chapters
Exodus	40 chapters
Numbers	36 chapters
2 Chronicles	36 chapters
Deuteronomy	34 chapters

❊ PSALMS THAT HAVE INSPIRED ❊ GREAT HYMNS OF THE CHURCH

Psalm	Hymn Title
8	"How Great Thou Art"
19	"For the Beauty of the Earth"
23	"Savior, Like a Shepherd Lead Us" "The King of Love My Shepherd Is" "Guide Me, O Thou Great Jehovah"
46	"A Mighty Fortress Is Our God" "It Is Well with My Soul"
48	"We Gather Together"
90	"O God, Our Help in Ages Past"
96	"Sing Praise to God Who Reigns Above"
100	"All People That on Earth Do Dwell"
121	"Abide with Me"
145	"O Worship the King"
148	"All Creatures of Our God and King" "This Is My Father's World"

❈ PARABLES ABOUT THE KINGDOM OF HEAVEN ❈

❈ THE ARK OF THE COVENANT ❈

The ark of the covenant was the holiest of Israel's sacred objects. It represented the Lord's presence. Mysterious events surrounded it.

■ When the Israelites reached Canaan, they had to cross the Jordan River to enter it. The priests led the way, carrying the ark. When they stepped into the river, the water upstream stopped flowing, which allowed the Israelites to cross the river on dry ground. When the priests stepped out of the riverbed, the water began flowing again (see Josh. 3).

■ The ark was so holy it was dangerous. The Philistines once captured the ark and placed it in the temple of their god Dagon. The next morning they found that Dagon's statue had fallen on its face, and its head and hands had broken off. Then the people of that region were afflicted with tumors and rats. Finally the Philistines sent the ark away by placing it on a cart pulled by two cows. Without any human guidance, the cows pulled the cart straight back to Israel (see 1 Sam. 5–6).

■ On another occasion, the ark was being brought to Jerusalem on a cart, and the oxen that were pulling the cart happened to stumble. The man who was guiding the cart touched the ark to steady it, and God struck him down. This made David afraid to bring the ark into the city, so he sent it to the house of another man. This time, however, the ark brought blessing to its keepers, so David changed his mind and joyfully retrieved the ark to complete its journey (see 2 Sam. 6).

❈ DISPUTED PASSAGES OF SCRIPTURE ❈

The origins of some Scripture passages have sparked a lot of debate. Were they part of the original book, or were they added later? Some manuscripts have them, some don't. Scholars have argued about the following examples for centuries:

Mark 16:9–20 • Luke 23:34 •
John 7:53–8:11 • Acts 8:37 • 1 John 5:7–8 •
Revelation 22:19

❈ THE COVENANTS OF GOD ❈

We use the term *covenant* today almost exclusively in legal and theological settings. In the Bible, a covenant indicated a solemn, binding agreement between two parties. The greatest significance of covenants in Scripture has to do with God's willingness to commit to agreements with humans. He keeps his promises to those who seem unable to keep theirs. Consider:

With Whom	Conditions	Reference
Adam	God will crush Satan and send a Savior.	Genesis 3:15
Noah	Never again will God use a flood to destroy the earth.	Genesis 8:21–22
Abraham	Abraham will have countless descendants who will possess the land of Canaan.	Genesis 12:2–3, 7
Moses	Moses and the Israelites will have God's provision and protection if they keep his commandments.	Exodus 19–24
David	God will provide an eternal and everlasting king from David's descendants.	2 Samuel 7:12–16
Christians	God will forgive his people and give new hearts to those willing to follow his commands.	Ezekiel 36:24–28

❄ JESUS ACCORDING TO JOHN ❄

John had a magnificent vision of Jesus while in exile on the Island of Patmos. This vision is recorded in the book of Revelation:

> I turned around to see the voice that was speaking to me. And when I turned I saw seven golden lampstands, and among the lampstands was someone "like a son of man," dressed in a robe reaching down to his feet and with a golden sash around his chest. His head and hair were white like wool, as white as snow, and his eyes were like blazing fire. His feet were like bronze glowing in a furnace, and his voice was like the sound of rushing waters. In his right hand he held seven stars, and out of his mouth came a sharp double-edged sword. His face was like the sun shining in all its brilliance.
>
> When I saw him, I fell at his feet as though dead. Then he placed his right hand on me and said: "Do not be afraid. I am the First and the Last. I am the Living One; I was dead, and behold I am alive for ever and ever! And I hold the keys of death and Hades." (1:12–18)

❄ NIGHTY-NIGHT ❄

I will lie down and sleep in peace,
for you alone, O LORD,
make me dwell in safety. (Ps. 4:8)

I lie down and sleep;
I wake again,
because the LORD sustains me. (Ps. 3:5)

In vain you rise early
and stay up late,
toiling for food to eat—
for he grants sleep to those he loves. (Ps. 127:2)

When you lie down, you will not be afraid;
when you lie down, your sleep will be sweet. (Prov. 3:24)

The sleep of a laborer is sweet,
whether he eats little or much,
but the abundance of a rich man
permits him no sleep. (Eccl. 5:12)

❧ THE SECOND LAW OF THERMODYNAMICS ❧
IN THE BIBLE

The second law of thermodynamics says energy in our universe is slowly being used up and eventually none will be left. In other words, the universe will eventually degenerate. The Bible makes it clear that the universe is indeed in this state.

- The creation waits in eager expectation for the sons of God to be revealed. For the creation was subjected to frustration, not by its own choice, but by the will of the one who subjected it, in hope that the creation itself will be liberated from its bondage to decay and brought into the glorious freedom of the children of God. We know that the whole creation has been groaning as in the pains of childbirth right up to the present time. (Rom. 8:19–22)

- In the beginning, O Lord, you laid the foundations of the earth, / and the heavens are the work of your hands. / They will perish, but you remain; / they will all wear out like a garment. / You will roll them up like a robe; / like a garment they will be changed. / But you remain the same, / and your years will never end. (Heb. 1:10–12)

❧ NOT JUST YOUR REGULAR JOES ❧

Joseph, son of Jacob . . . . He was a dream interpreter who was sold as a slave by his brothers, put into jail, and eventually overcame it all to become the right-hand man of the pharaoh (Gen. 37–50).

Joseph, earthly father of Jesus . . . . Joseph was betrothed to Mary when she became pregnant with Jesus. He acted as the earthly father to Jesus (Matt. 1–2).

Joseph of Arimathea . . . . He was a disciple of Jesus. He was also the one who put Jesus's body in a tomb after he was killed (John 19:38–42).

Joseph, called Justus . . . . The disciples cast lots between Joseph and Matthias to decide who would become the twelfth apostle (Acts 1:23–26).

Joseph, called Barnabas . . . . Barnabas sold a field and gave the money to the apostles (Acts 4:36–37).

Prophet	Message
Hosea	Israel has been unfaithful to God and will be judged, but God's love for its people will continue and he will restore them.
Joel	God's people must repent. The Lord is coming and the nations will be judged.
Amos	God will judge the people for their complacent worship and their idolatry.
Obadiah	Anyone who opposes God's people (specifically Edom) will be judged.
Jonah	God's mercy can reach even the worst of sinners, and God is completely free—he can be bound by nothing.
Micah	God hates sin but delights in mercy and forgiveness.
Nahum	God will punish Nineveh for its wickedness.
Habakkuk	God is sovereign over all things. Even when evil seems to be winning, God is in complete control.
Zephaniah	God will judge and punish his people, but afterward he will graciously restore them.
Haggai	God's temple, which represents God's presence, must be rebuilt.
Zechariah	God's people have hope of a future deliverance by the coming Messiah.
Malachi	God's people must turn away from their sin and give themselves to God.

❧ FASHION STATEMENT ❧

Even in biblical times, many of the people were concerned about fashion. Here are a few of the items they used to enhance their beauty.

Nose ring (Genesis 24:22) • Bracelet
(Genesis 24:30) • Necklace (Ezekiel 16:11) •
Eye shadow (Ezekiel 23:40) • Gold chain (Daniel 5:7) •
Earring (Judges 8:24) • Garland (Proverbs 1:9) • Ankle
chains (Isaiah 3:20) • Perfume (Nehemiah 3:8) •
Strings of jewels (Song 1:10) • Ring
(Exodus 35:22) • Cosmetics
(Esther 2:12) • Crown
(Ezekiel 16:12)

❀ RESURRECTIONS ❀

Who	How	Where
The son of the widow in Zarephath	Raised by Elijah	1 Kings 17:21–22
The son of the Shunammite woman	Raised by Elisha	2 Kings 4:34–35
An unidentified dead man	By coming into contact with Elisha's bones	2 Kings 13:20–21
The daughter of Jairus	Raised by Jesus	Luke 8:54–55
The son of the widow in Nain	Raised by Jesus	Luke 7:14–15
Lazarus of Bethany	Raised by Jesus	John 11:43–44
Dorcas of Joppa	Raised by Peter	Acts 9:40
Eutychus of Troas	Raised by Paul	Acts 20:10–12
Jesus, the Son of God	Raised by God the Father—never to die again	Matthew 28; Mark 16; Luke 24; John 20–21

❀ TWO MEN WHO NEVER DIED ❀

Two biblical figures, Elijah and Enoch, never experienced death. God saw fit to take them to heaven before they passed away. The following passages detail these amazing stories.

Elijah . . . . As they [Elijah and Elisha] were walking along and talking together, suddenly a chariot of fire and horses of fire appeared and separated the two of them, and Elijah went up to heaven in a whirlwind. Elisha saw this and cried out, "My father! My father! The chariots and horsemen of Israel!" And Elisha saw him no more. (2 Kings 2:11–12)

Enoch . . . . When Enoch had lived 65 years, he became the father of Methuselah. And after he became the father of Methuselah, Enoch walked with God 300 years and had other sons and daughters. Altogether, Enoch lived 365 years. Enoch walked with God; then he was no more, because God took him away. (Gen. 5:21–24)

By faith Enoch was taken from this life, so that he did not experience death; he could not be found, because God had taken him away. For before he was taken, he was commended as one who pleased God. (Heb. 11:5)

❧ THE BOW AND ARROW ❧

The bow and arrow were a common weapon in biblical times. Here are some examples of bow-and-arrow attacks:

- He shall surely be stoned or shot with arrows; not a hand is to be laid on him. Whether man or animal, he shall not be permitted to live. (Exod. 19:13)

- Then the archers shot arrows at your servants from the wall, and some of the king's men died. Moreover, your servant Uriah the Hittite is dead. (2 Sam. 11:24)

- Then Jehu drew his bow and shot Joram between the shoulders. The arrow pierced his heart and he slumped down in his chariot. (2 Kings 9:24)

- These were the men who came to David at Ziklag, while he was banished from the presence of Saul son of Kish (they were among the warriors who helped him in battle; they were armed with bows and were able to shoot arrows or to sling stones right-handed or left-handed; they were kinsmen of Saul from the tribe of Benjamin). (1 Chron. 12:1–2)

- In Jerusalem he made machines designed by skillful men for use on the towers and on the corner defenses to shoot arrows and hurl large stones. His fame spread far and wide, for he was greatly helped until he became powerful. (2 Chron. 26:15)

- Take up your positions around Babylon, / all you who draw the bow. / Shoot at her! Spare no arrows, / for she has sinned against the LORD. (Jer. 50:14)

❧ NOW, THAT'S A GOOD QUESTION ❧

- Whom have I in heaven but you? (Ps. 73:25)

- Will a man rob God? (Mal. 3:8)

- Who has understood the mind of the LORD, / or instructed him as his counselor? (Isa. 40:13)

- Why embrace the bosom of another man's wife? (Prov. 5:20)

- Who do people say the Son of Man is? (Matt. 16:13)

- Which is easier: to say to the paralytic, "Your sins are forgiven," or to say, "Get up, take your mat and walk"? (Mark 2:9)

- What then? Shall we sin because we are not under law but under grace? (Rom. 6:15)

- If God is for us, who can be against us? (Rom. 8:31)

- Who knows but that you have come to royal position for such a time as this? (Esther 4:14)

- Where can I flee from your presence? (Ps. 139:7)

- How long will you waiver between two opinions? (1 Kings 18:21)

- Can the Ethiopian change his skin / or the leopard its spots? (Jer. 13:23)

- Could you men not keep watch with me for one hour? (Matt. 26:40)

- How can a man be born when he is old? (John 3:4)

- What must I do to be saved? (Acts 16:30)

- Who will rescue me from this body of death? (Rom. 7:24)

- Who shall separate us from the love of Christ? (Rom. 8:35)

❧ THE MIGHTIEST OF MEN ❧

Here are a few of King David's mighty men:

Name	Accomplishment	Reference
Josheb-Basshebeth	Used a spear to kill eight hundred men in one encounter.	2 Samuel 23:8
Eleazer	Struck down the Philistines until his hand grew tired and clung to his sword.	2 Samuel 23:9–10

Name	Accomplishment	Reference
Shammah	The Philistines gathered together in a field, and Israel's troops ran away from them. Shammah stood his ground in the middle of the field and killed the Philistines.	2 Samuel 23:11–12
Abishai	Killed three hundred men with a spear.	2 Samuel 23:18
Benaiah	Went into a pit on a snowy day and killed a lion. He also killed a huge Egyptian by grabbing his own spear and using it to kill him.	2 Samuel 23:20–21

❅ COLORS IN THE BIBLE ❅

Color	References	Symbolism
Red	Isaiah 1:15, 18; 63:1–6; Zechariah 6:2; Hebrews 9:19; Revelation 12:3	Blood, war
Yellow	Psalm 68:13; Leviticus 13:30, 32	None
Green	Genesis 1:30; Psalm 23:2; Isaiah 15:6; Jeremiah 17:8; Ezekiel 17:24; Hosea 14:8	Life, growth, rest
Blue	Exodus 24:10, 26:1, 28:31; Numbers 15:38; Jeremiah 10:8–9; Ezekiel 1:26	Wealth, heaven
Purple	Judges 8:26; Proverbs 31:22; Jeremiah 10:9; Mark 15:17, 20; Revelation 17:4	Wealth, royalty
Black	Lamentations 4:8; Zechariah 6:2, 6; 2 Peter 2:17; Revelation 6:5, 12	Disease, death, judgment
Gray	Genesis 42:38	Age
White	Psalm 51:7; Daniel 7:9; Mark 16:5; Revelation 1:14; 4:4; 19:11	Purity, holiness, forgiveness

❈ RUNNING THROUGH THE BIBLE ❈

Here are some characters who would have appreciated a good pair of Nikes:

- But Esau ran to meet Jacob and embraced him; he threw his arms around his neck and kissed him. And they wept. (Gen. 33:4)
- She caught him by his cloak and said, "Come to bed with me!" But he left his cloak in her hand and ran out of the house. (Gen. 39:12)
- Elisha said to Gehazi, "Tuck your cloak into your belt, take my staff in your hand and run. If you meet anyone, do not greet him, and if anyone greets you, do not answer. Lay my staff on the boy's face." (2 Kings 4:29)
- Ahimaaz son of Zadok again said to Joab, "Come what may, please let me run behind the Cushite." But Joab replied, "My son, why do you want to go? You don't have any news that will bring you a reward." He said, "Come what may, I want to run." So Joab said, "Run!" Then Ahimaaz ran by way of the plain and outran the Cushite. (2 Sam. 18:22–23)
- As the Philistine moved closer to attack him, David ran quickly toward the battle line to meet him. (1 Sam. 17:48)
- The power of the LORD came upon Elijah and, tucking his cloak into his belt, he ran ahead of Ahab all the way to Jezreel. (1 Kings 18:46)
- So he got up and went to his father. But while he was still a long way off, his father saw him and was filled with compassion for him; he ran to his son, threw his arms around him and kissed him. (Luke 15:20)

❈ THE GLORY OF GOD IN THE OLD TESTAMENT ❈

- A cherubim wielding a flaming, flashing sword at the entrance to Eden (Gen. 3).
- The burning bush (Exod. 3).
- Smoke billowed from Mount Sinai as it trembled violently (Exod. 19).
- A glow on Moses's face (Exod. 34).
- The ark of the covenant represented God's presence (Exod. 37).
- A pillar of cloud that led the Israelites in the wilderness by day (Exod. 40).
- A pillar of fire that led the Israelites in the wilderness by night (Exod. 40).
- A gentle whisper that Elijah heard after an earthquake, a mighty wind, and a blazing fire (1 Kings 19).
- Smoke in the temple complete with seraphs chanting and the thresholds shaking (Isa. 6).
- The fourth man in the fiery furnace with Shadrach, Meshach, and Abednego (Dan. 3).

❦ GIVE CREDIT WHERE CREDIT IS DUE: ❦
WHO WROTE WHAT PARTS OF THE BIBLE

Author	Book
Moses	Genesis
	Exodus
	Leviticus
	Numbers
	Deuteronomy
	Job
Joshua	Joshua
Isaiah	Isaiah
Jeremiah	1 Kings
	2 Kings
	Jeremiah
	Lamentations
Ezra	1 Chronicles
	2 Chronicles
	Ezra
	Nehemiah
Samuel/Nathan/Gad	Judges
	Ruth
	1 Samuel
	2 Samuel
Mostly David	Psalms
Unknown, possibly Mordecai	Esther
Solomon	Proverbs
	Ecclesiastes
	Song of Solomon
Ezekiel	Ezekiel
Daniel	Daniel
Hosea	Hosea
Joel	Joel
Amos	Amos
Obadiah	Obadiah
Jonah	Jonah
Micah	Micah

Author	Book
Nahum	Nahum
Habakkuk	Habakkuk
Zephaniah	Zephaniah
Haggai	Haggai
Zechariah	Zechariah
Malachi	Malachi
Matthew	Matthew
Mark	Mark
John	John
	1 John
	2 John
	3 John
	Revelation
Paul	Romans
	1 Corinthians
	2 Corinthians
	Galatians
	Ephesians
	Philippians
	Colossians
	1 Thessalonians
	2 Thessalonians
	1 Timothy
	2 Timothy
	Titus
Luke	Luke
	Acts
Unknown, possibly Paul	Hebrews
James	James
Peter	1 Peter
	2 Peter
Philemon	Philemon
Jude	Jude

❊ LEARNING LESSONS FROM SILVER ❊

Here is a sampling of the way the Bible uses silver to teach spiritual lessons:

- The words of the LORD are pure words: as silver tried in a furnace of earth, purified seven times. (Ps. 12:6 KJV)

- For thou, O God, hast proved us: thou hast tried us, as silver is tried. (Ps. 66:10 KJV)

- The law of thy mouth is better unto me than thousands of gold and silver. (Ps. 119:72 KJV)

- And if you call out for insight / and cry aloud for understanding, / and if you look for it as for silver / and search for it as for hidden treasure, / then you will understand the fear of the LORD / and find the knowledge of God. (Prov. 2:3–5)

- Choose my instruction instead of silver, / knowledge rather than choice gold. (Prov. 8:10)

- How much better to get wisdom than gold, / to choose understanding rather than silver! (Prov. 16:16)

- The crucible for silver and the furnace for gold, / but the LORD tests the heart. (Prov. 17:3)

- He who loves silver will not be satisfied with silver; / nor he who loves abundance, with increase. / This also is vanity. (Eccl. 5:10 NKJV)

❊ ENGINES IN THE BIBLE? ❊

One biblical figure, Uzziah, was incredibly creative and inventive, but he let it go to his head.

And Uzziah prepared for all the army shields, spears, helmets, coats of mail, bows, and stones for slinging. In Jerusalem he made engines, invented by skillful men, to be on the towers and the corners, to shoot arrows and great stones. And his fame spread far, for he was marvelously helped, till he was strong.

But when he was strong, he grew proud, to his destruction. For he was unfaithful to the LORD his God and entered the temple of the LORD to burn incense on the altar of incense. But Azariah the priest went in after him, with eighty priests of the LORD who were men of valor, and they withstood

King Uzziah and said to him, "It is not for you, Uzziah, to burn incense to the LORD, but for the priests the sons of Aaron, who are consecrated to burn incense. Go out of the sanctuary, for you have done wrong, and it will bring you no honor from the LORD God."

Then Uzziah was angry. Now he had a censer in his hand to burn incense, and when he became angry with the priests, leprosy broke out on his forehead in the presence of the priests in the house of the LORD, by the altar of incense. And Azariah the chief priest and all the priests looked at him, and behold, he was leprous in his forehead! And they rushed him out quickly, and he himself hurried to go out, because the LORD had struck him. (2 Chron. 26:14–20 ESV)

❀ WHO IS MELCHIZEDEK? ❀

Melchizedek is one of the most mysterious figures in the Bible. Who was he, and where did he come from? Here's a profile from the few tidbits we're given:

- He was a king of Salem (Gen. 14:18).

- He was a priest of *El-Elyon*, God Most High (Gen. 14:18).

- He first appears in Scripture after Abram had just rescued Lot and his possessions from King Kedorlaomer. He brought Abram bread and wine and blessed him, and Abram gave him a tenth of the items he took back during his rescue (Gen. 14:17–20; Heb. 7:1–2).

- He was part of a priestly order that was separate from Aaron's priesthood. The writer of Hebrews notes a number of signs that it was a superior order (Heb. 7:1–14).

- Abraham is a lesser person than Melchizedek (Heb. 7:1–7).

- Levi, Abraham's ancestor, honored Melchizedek by paying him a tithe (Levi was "still in the body of [Abraham]") (Heb. 7:9–10).

- In the order of Melchizedek, a person could be declared a priest eternally by an oath from God (Ps. 110:4).

- Jesus was a priest in the order of Melchizedek. In fact, he was a high priest in this order (Heb. 5:1–10; 7:15–28).

❀ THE AILMENTS JESUS CURED ❀

Demon-possessed—Matthew 4:23–24; 8:16, 28–34; 9:32–34; 15:21–28;
17:14–18; Mark 1:23–26, 32–34

Epileptic—Matthew 4:23–24; 17:14–18

Paralytic—Matthew 4:23–24; 8:5–13; 9:1–8; 15:29–31; Mark 2:3–12

Leprous—Matthew 8:2–4; Mark 1:40–45

Sick with a Fever—Matthew 8:14–15; Mark 1:29–31

Bleeding—Matthew 9:20–22

Death—Matthew 9:18–26

Blind—Matthew 9:27–31; 15:29–31; 20:29–34; 21:14

Mute—Matthew 9:32–34; 15:29–31

Withered Hand—Matthew 12:9–14; Mark 3:1–5

Hungry—Matthew 14:13–21; 15:32–39

Lame—Matthew 15:29–31; 21:14

Deaf—Mark 7:31–37

Unable to Speak Properly—Mark 7:31–37

❀ SPEAKING IN TONGUES ❀

Ever wonder what the Bible says about speaking in tongues?

- For anyone who speaks in a tongue does not speak to men but to God. Indeed, no one understands him; he utters mysteries with his spirit. But everyone who prophesies speaks to men for their strengthening, encouragement and comfort. He who speaks in a tongue edifies himself, but he who prophesies edifies the church. I would like every one of you to speak in tongues, but I would rather have you prophesy. He who prophesies is greater than one who speaks in tongues, unless he interprets, so that the church may be edified. (1 Cor. 14:2–5)

- I thank God that I speak in tongues more than all of you. But in the church I would rather speak five intelligible words to instruct others than ten thousand words in a tongue. (1 Cor. 14:18–19)

- What then shall we say, brothers? When you come together, everyone has a hymn, or a word of instruction, a revelation, a tongue or an interpretation. All of these must be done for the strengthening of the church. If anyone speaks in a tongue, two—or at the most three—should speak, one at a time, and someone must interpret. If there is no interpreter, the speaker should keep quiet in the church and speak to himself and God. (1 Cor. 14:26–28)

▨ Therefore, my brothers, be eager to prophesy, and do not forbid speaking in tongues. But everything should be done in a fitting and orderly way. (1 Cor. 14:39–40)

❈ ALL THE HERODS ❈

References to Herod in the New Testament are sometimes confusing. What started as a name quickly became a family title. The first Herod (the Great) received the designation "King of the Jews" from Rome though he was not of royal blood. He and his family ruthlessly ruled Israel during Jesus's life and the days of the early Christian Church. They are listed chronologically below:

Herod	*What He Is Known For*	*Reference*
Herod the Great	He attempted to murder Jesus by issuing a decree to have all male children, age two and under, in the Bethlehem area killed.	Matthew 2:13, 16
Herod Antipas	He ridiculed and mocked Jesus while he was in custody before his crucifixion. He also had John the Baptist beheaded.	Luke 23:6–12; Matthew 14:1–12
Herod Agrippa I	He had James executed. Also, when the people called him a god, he did not give praise to God, so he immediately was eaten by worms and died.	Acts 12:1–2, 21–23
Herod Agrippa II	Paul made his defense before him at Caesarea.	Acts 25:13–26:32

❀ PHRASES TAKEN FROM THE BIBLE ❀
THAT ARE STILL USED TODAY

The English language is filled with popular idioms and expressions that are taken from the King James Version of the Bible. Even though the KJV is a translation that sounds more like a Shakespearean play than everyday vernacular, many of its lovely phrases have become embedded in common speech. People on the street speak biblical phrases daily without realizing they are doing so. For example:

Rise and shine (Isa. 60:1).
Give up the ghost (Luke 23:46 KJV).
By the skin of your teeth (Job 19:20).
See eye to eye (Isa. 52:8 KJV).
Safe and sound (Luke 15:27).
Eat, drink, and be merry (Luke 12:19).
An eye for an eye (Matt. 5:38).
Scapegoat (Lev. 16:8, 10, 26).
The first will be last (Matt. 19:30).
A thorn in the flesh (2 Cor. 12:7).
Eye of a needle (Matt. 19:24).

Other expressions have become common parlance in our culture that are identifiable as being biblical in nature, even though they are not taken from the King James Version:

Love covers a multitude of sins (1 Pet. 4:8).
The greatest of these is love (1 Cor. 13:13).
The devil made me do it (Gen. 3:13).
A cross to bear (Matt. 16:24).
The log in your eye (Matt. 7:4).

❀ ARAMAIC PHRASES IN THE NEW TESTAMENT ❀

When the Babylonians took the Jews into exile in 586 BC, the Jews learned to speak Aramaic instead of Hebrew. Six hundred years later, Aramaic was the language of Israel, and thus Jesus spoke it. Although Greek replaced Aramaic as the official language of the Middle East after the coming of Alexander the Great, Aramaic gave way to Arabic in the seventh century AD, following the rise of Islam. Curiously, there are Aramaic phrases peppered in the Greek text of the New Testament.

❦ ARAMAIC PHRASES IN THE ❦ NEW TESTAMENT—CONT.

Aramaic Phrase	Meaning	Reference
Eloi, Eloi, lama sabachthani	My God, my God, why have you forsaken me?	Matthew 27:46
Talitha koum	Little girl, I say to you, get up!	Mark 5:41
Ephphatha	Be opened!	Mark 7:34
Cephas	Peter	John 1:42
Mammon	Worldly riches	Matthew 6:24 (KJV)
Abba	Daddy	Romans 8:15
Maranatha	Come, O Lord!	1 Corinthians 16:22 (KJV)

❦ WHO IS THE HOLY SPIRIT? ❦

- *The Holy Spirit is God. He can be blasphemed against:*
  "But whoever blasphemes against the Holy Spirit will never be forgiven; he is guilty of an eternal sin" (Mark 3:29).

- *The Holy Spirit is omnipresent:*
  "Where can I go from your Spirit? / Where can I flee from your presence?" (Ps. 139:7).

- *The Holy Spirit is a person. He can be grieved:*
  "Yet they rebelled / and grieved his Holy Spirit" (Isa. 63:10).

- *The Holy Spirit is a teacher:*
  "But the Counselor, the Holy Spirit, whom the Father will send in my name, will teach you all things and will remind you of everything I have said to you" (John 14:26).

- *The Holy Spirit is a revealer and glorifier of Jesus:*
  "He will bring glory to me by taking from what is mine and making it known to you. All that belongs to the Father is mine. That is why I said the Spirit will take from what is mine and make it known to you" (John 16:14–15).

❧ BIBLICAL WOMEN NAMED MARY ❧

For Christians the world over, the mention of the name Mary conjures up thoughts of the woman whose virgin womb carried the Son of God. But although Mary the mother of Jesus is the most prominent, she is not the only one to claim that name.

- Naomi, who buried a husband and two sons in Moab before returning to her husband's hometown of Bethlehem in Judah with her daughter-in-law Ruth. There she referred to herself as **"Mara"** (or Mary), which means "bitter" (Ruth 1:20).

- **Mary the wife of Cleopas** (John 19:25) was at the foot of the cross with Mary of Magdala and Mary the mother of Jesus as the Savior died. An examination of Matthew 27:56 and Mark 15:40 suggests that she is also referred to as "Mary the **mother of James** and Joses," who was the "other Mary" who went to the tomb to anoint the body of Jesus (Matt. 28:1).

- **Mary of Magdala** (Mary Magdalene) appears in Luke 8:3 as one of the women who "ministered to Christ of their substance" (KJV). Jesus cast seven demons out of this Mary. She became a faithful follower and was the first to witness Jesus's resurrection.

- **Mary the sister of Martha** lived in Bethany with their brother, Lazarus. In contrast to Martha, who was concerned about household details when Jesus was their guest, Mary was content to sit at Jesus' feet and enjoy his presence (Luke 10). And speaking of the Lord's feet, on the occasion of his final visit to Bethany, this is the Mary who anointed Jesus with a very costly ointment in the home of a former leper by the name of Simon (Mark 14:3; John 12:2–3). (Note: Although many believe that the Mary who sat at Jesus's feet is the same Mary who anointed Jesus, this information has not been proved conclusively.)

- **Mary the mother of John Mark** was one of the first disciples (Acts 12:12). According to Colossians 4:10, Mark was the cousin of Barnabas. This would mean that Mary was Barnabas's aunt, and she joined with him in disposing of their land and giving the proceeds of the sale into the treasury of the church (Acts 4:37; 12:12). She made her home in Jerusalem available as a gathering place for the disciples.

- **Mary in the church at Rome** was mentioned by Paul in his acknowledgments at the end of his letter to the Romans. This Mary worked very hard for the church in Rome (Rom. 16:6).

❦ A HORSE IS A HORSE, OF COURSE, OF COURSE ❦

A small selection of unique "horse" passages:

- He was brought back by horse and was buried in Jerusalem with his fathers, in the City of David. (2 Kings 14:20)
- Have them bring a royal robe the king has worn and a horse the king has ridden, one with a royal crest placed on its head. Then let the robe and horse be entrusted to one of the king's most noble princes. Let them robe the man the king delights to honor, and lead him on the horse through the city streets, proclaiming before him, "This is what is done for the man the king delights to honor!" (Esther 6:8–9)
- The horse is made ready for the day of battle, / but victory rests with the LORD. (Prov. 21:31)
- During the night I had a vision—and there before me was a man riding a red horse! He was standing among the myrtle trees in a ravine. Behind him were red, brown and white horses. (Zech. 1:8)
- "On that day I will strike every horse with panic and its rider with madness," declares the LORD. "I will keep a watchful eye over the house of Judah, but I will blind all the horses of the nations." (Zech. 12:4)
- I looked, and there before me was a white horse! Its rider held a bow, and he was given a crown, and he rode out as a conqueror bent on conquest. (Rev. 6:2)
- I saw heaven standing open and there before me was a white horse, whose rider is called Faithful and True. With justice he judges and makes war. (Rev. 19:11)

❦ WEATHER IN THE BIBLE ❦

Whirlwind	Nahum 1:3	Thunderstorm	Isaiah 30:30
Storm	Job 38:1	Flooding downpour	Isaiah 28:2
Wind	Exodus 10:19	Mist	Isaiah 44:22
Thunder	Exodus 9:28	Stormy winds	Psalm 148:8
Snow	Psalm 147:16	Rain	Genesis 7:4
Frost	Psalm 147:16	Drought	Jeremiah 50:38
Hail	Psalm 105:32	Hurricane force winds	Acts 27:14

❈ BETTER THAN GOLD ❈

The Scriptures declare that a few things are more valuable than gold:

- A good name is more desirable than great riches; / to be esteemed is better than silver or gold. (Prov. 22:1)

- The law from your mouth is more precious to me / than thousands of pieces of silver and gold. (Ps. 119:72)

- How much better to get wisdom than gold, / to choose understanding rather than silver! (Prov. 16:16)

- Choose my instruction instead of silver, / knowledge rather than choice gold, / for wisdom is more precious than rubies, / and nothing you desire can compare with her. (Prov. 8:10–11)

- Because I love your commands / more than gold, more than pure gold, / and because I consider all your precepts right, / I hate every wrong path. (Ps. 119:127–128)

- The fear of the LORD is pure, / enduring forever. / The ordinances of the LORD are sure / and altogether righteous. / They are more precious than gold, / than much pure gold; / they are sweeter than honey, / than honey from the comb. (Ps. 19:9–10)

- For you know that it was not with perishable things such as silver or gold that you were redeemed from the empty way of life handed down to you from your forefathers, but with the precious blood of Christ, a lamb without blemish or defect. (1 Pet. 1:18–19)

- These have come so that your faith—of greater worth than gold, which perishes even though refined by fire—may be proved genuine and may result in praise, glory and honor when Jesus Christ is revealed. (1 Pet. 1:7)

❈ PRAYERS: SHORTEST AND LONGEST ❈

The shortest prayer recorded in the Bible, "Lord, save me!"
was uttered by Peter when he began to sink in the stormy seas
as he was walking out to Jesus on the water (Matt. 14:30).

The longest prayer recorded in the Bible is Solomon's
prayer dedicating the Temple (1 Kings 8:23–53).
His prayer is 1,219 words long.

❋ FAMOUS MURDERS ❋

Cain killed Abel (Gen. 4:8).

Lamech killed a young man (Gen. 4:23).

Simeon and Levi killed Hamor, Shechem, and all the living males of the city (Gen. 34:25–26).

Moses killed an Egyptian (Exod. 2:12).

Ehud killed King Eglon of Moab (Judg. 3:21).

Jael killed Sisera (Judg. 4:21).

Joab killed Abner (2 Sam. 3:27).

Recab and Baanah killed Ish-Bosheth (2 Sam. 4:6).

David had Uriah killed (2 Sam. 11:15–17).

Absalom had his brothers kill Amnon (2 Sam. 13:28–29).

Joab and his men killed Absalom (2 Sam. 18:14–15).

Joab killed Amasa (2 Sam. 20:10).

Zimri killed Elah (1 Kings 16:10).

Jezebel had Naboth killed (1 Kings 21:10, 13).

Hazael killed Ben-Hadad (2 Kings 8:15).

Jehu killed Jehoram (2 Kings 9:24).

Jehu had Ahaziah killed (2 Kings 9:27).

Jehu killed Jezebel (2 Kings 9:33).

Servants killed Joash (2 Kings 12:20–21).

Shallum killed Zechariah (2 Kings 15:10).

Menahem killed Shallum (2 Kings 15:14).

Pekah killed Pekahiah (2 Kings 15:25).

Hoshea killed Pekah (2 Kings 15:30).

Servants killed Amon (2 Kings 21:23).

Ishmael killed Gedaliah (2 Kings 25:25).

Joash killed Zechariah the high priest (2 Chron. 24:21–22).

Nebuchadnezzar killed the sons of Zedekiah (Jer. 39:6).

King Herod killed male babies in Bethlehem (Matt. 2:16).

Herodias had John the Baptist killed (Mark 6:24, 27).

The Jewish leaders killed Stephen (Acts 7:57–60).

❄ I TELL YOU THE TRUTH! ❄

Jesus states "I tell you the truth" 76 times throughout the four Gospels. Below are the references where you can find each of his "truth" statements.

Matthew 5:18	Matthew 21:31	Mark 13:30	John 5:24–25
Matthew 5:26	Matthew 23:36	Mark 14:9	John 6:26
Matthew 6:2	Matthew 24:2	Mark 14:18	John 6:32
Matthew 6:5	Matthew 24:34	Mark 14:25	John 6:47
Matthew 6:16	Matthew 24:47	Mark 14:30	John 6:53
Matthew 8:10	Matthew 25:12	Luke 4:24	John 8:34
Matthew 10:15	Matthew 25:40	Luke 9:27	John 8:51
Matthew 10:23	Matthew 25:45	Luke 12:37	John 8:58
Matthew 10:42	Matthew 26:13	Luke 12:44	John 10:1
Matthew 11:11	Matthew 26:21	Luke 18:17	John 10:7
Matthew 13:17	Matthew 26:34	Luke 18:29	John 12:24
Matthew 16:28	Mark 3:28	Luke 21:3	John 13:16
Matthew 17:20	Mark 8:12	Luke 21:32	John 13:20–21
Matthew 18:3	Mark 9:1	Luke 23:43	John 13:38
Matthew 18:13	Mark 9:41	John 1:51	John 14:12
Matthew 18:18	Mark 10:15	John 3:3	John 16:7
Matthew 19:23	Mark 10:29	John 3:5	John 16:20
Matthew 19:28	Mark 11:23	John 3:11	John 16:23
Matthew 21:21	Mark 12:43	John 5:19	John 21:18

❈ ABOMINATION! ❈

An abomination is a person, thing, or action that causes a response of extreme disgust or hatred. The following is a list of things that God considers abomination.

Men having sex with other men. (Leviticus 18:22; 20:13 KJV)

Graven images of other gods. (Deuteronomy 7:25–26 KJV)

Burning your sons or daughters in fire for other gods. (Deuteronomy 12:31 KJV)

Serving other gods. (Deuteronomy 13:12–14 KJV)

Sacrificing a blemished animal. (Deuteronomy 17:1 KJV)

Worshiping other gods such as the sun, moon, and stars.
(Deuteronomy 17:3–4 KJV)

Divination, fortune telling, sorcery, being a medium or a necromancer.
(Deuteronomy 18:9–12 ESV)

Men dressing like women or women dressing like men. (Deuteronomy 22:5 KJV)

Bringing the wages of a prostitute into the house of God.
(Deuteronomy 23:18 KJV)

Remarrying a woman that you previously divorced (if she married someone else
after you divorced her). (Deuteronomy 24:4 KJV)

Dishonesty. (Deuteronomy 25:13–16 KJV; Proverbs 12:22 KJV)

The person who makes idols. (Deuteronomy 27:15 KJV)

Haughty eyes. (Proverbs 6:16–19 ESV)

A lying tongue. (Proverbs 6:16–19 ESV)

Hands that shed innocent blood. (Proverbs 6:16–19 KJV)

A heart that devises wicked plans. (Proverbs 6:16–19 KJV)

Feet that make haste to run to evil. (Proverbs 6:16–19 ESV)

A false witness who breathes out lies. (Proverbs 6:16–19 ESV)

One who sows discord among brothers. (Proverbs 6:16–19 ESV)

The sacrifice of the wicked. (Proverbs 15:8–9 KJV)

The thoughts of the wicked. (Proverbs 15:26 KJV)

Those that are prideful. (Proverbs 16:5 KJV)

One who justifies the wicked and condemns the just. (Proverbs 17:15 KJV)

The prayer of those who turn their ears away from hearing the law.
(Proverbs 28:9 KJV)

❀ THE KING OF BEASTS ❀

Proverbs 30:30 states that the lion is the "mightiest among beasts, and does not turn away from any." The following is a list of passages that pertain to the "king of beasts."

- Samson tore a lion apart with his bare hands. (Judges 14:5–6)

- When David was young, he killed lions that tried to harm the sheep he was shepherding. He killed them by grabbing them by the hair and striking them. (1 Samuel 17:34–37)

- Benaiah son of Jehoiada, a valiant fighter from Kabzeel, went into a pit on a snowy day and killed a lion. (2 Samuel 23:20)

- A lion killed a man of God and threw his body down on the road. (1 Kings 13:20–30)

- One of the sons of the prophets commanded a man he was with to strike him with his weapon. When the man refused to do so, the prophet told him that he would be killed by a lion for disobeying the Lord. The man left and was killed by a lion. (1 Kings 20:35–36)

- The people living in Samaria did not worship the Lord, so he sent lions into the town to kill some of the people. (2 Kings 17:25–26)

- Isaiah prophesied that in the coming kingdom, the lion and the calf will lie down together, and a little child will lead them. The prophesy also states that lions will eat straw like an ox. (Isaiah 11:6–7)

- Daniel was thrown into a den of lions for praying to God. Daniel was protected by God—the lions did not harm him. (Daniel 6:16–24)

- Daniel had a vision of four great beasts coming up out of the sea. One of them was like a lion with the wings of an eagle. (Daniel 7:4)

- Peter states that the devil is like a "roaring lion looking for someone to devour." (1 Peter 5:8)

- Jesus is called the Lion of the tribe of Judah. (Revelation 5:5)

❧ THE FINAL JUDGMENT ❧

What will the final judgment be like? Here are a number of passages that reveal information on what will take place.

Event	*Reference*
Jesus will be the Judge.	Acts 10:42
The secrets of men's hearts will be judged.	Romans 2:16; 1 Corinthians 4:5
Everyone will stand before the judgment seat.	Romans 14:10
Jesus will come in his Father's glory and reward each person according to what he has done.	Matthew 16:27
Everyone will stand before the throne.	Revelation 20:12–13
Jesus will separate the sheep from the goats.	Matthew 25:31–36
Only those whose names are written in the book of life will be saved.	Revelation 20:15
Everyone will die and face judgment once.	Hebrews 9:27
The quality of each Christian's work will be tested.	1 Corinthians 3:10–15
Teachers of God's truth will be judged more strictly.	James 3:1
Christians will be judged by the law that gives freedom.	James 2:12
Christians are justified by the blood of Jesus, who will rescue them from the coming wrath.	Romans 5:9; 1 Thessalonians 1:10; 1 Thessalonians 5:9
Christians will judge angels.	1 Corinthians 6:3

SOURCES

All the Herods

Adapted from: Wayne Blank, "The Herods," Daily Bible Study,
http://www.keyway.ca/htm2002/herods.htm.

A Baker's Dozen

Adapted from: George B. Eager, "Bread," *The International Standard Bible Encyclopedia*, ed. Geoffrey William Bromiley,
http://www.bible.org/isbe.asp?id=1681.

The Beatitudes in the Book of Revelation

Adapted from: Don Fortner, "Our Lord's Final Beatitudes," *Pictures of Christ in Revelation*, http://www.freegrace.net/dfbooks/dfrevbk/rev52.htm.

Colors in the Bible

Adapted from: Walter Elwell, ed., *Evangelical Dictionary of Biblical Theology* (Grand Rapids, Mich.: Baker; Carlisle, Cumbria: Paternoster),
http://bible.crosswalk.com/Dictionaries BakersEvangelicalDictionary/.
"Color Symbolism in the Bible," RidingTheBeast.com,
http://www.ridingthebeast.com/articles/colors/.

Confirmed Prophetic Occurrences

Adapted from: Josh McDowell, *Evidence That Demands a Verdict: Historical Evidences for the Christian Faith,* vol. 1 (San Bernardino, Calif.: Here's Life, 1979), 267–323.

DEAD MEN WALKING

Adapted from: H. L. Willmington, *Willmington's Book of Bible Lists* (Wheaton, Ill.: Tyndale House Publishers, Inc., 1987), 199–208.

DISPUTED PASSAGES OF SCRIPTURE

Adapted from: C. Pope, "Comparing Bible Translations," Realms of Faith, http://faith.propadeutic.com/questions.html.

FAMOUS EXCUSES

Adapted from: Willmington, *Willmington's Book*, 103.

FAMOUS LAST WORDS

Adapted from: Randy Walker, e-mail to Inspirations mailing list, January 17, 2000, http://lists.spunge.org/inspirations/archive/msg00215.html.

GODLESS SONS OF GODLY FATHERS

Adapted from: David Wurm, ed., "Chronology of Israel's Kings and Prophets," *The Book: Interactive Bible Studies* (revision date: March 12, 2005), http://www.thebookwurm.com/kingchrt.htm.

GODLY SONS OF GODLESS FATHERS

Adapted from: Wurm, "Chronology," http://www.thebookwurm.com/kingchrt.htm.

GONE TO THE DOGS

Adapted from: Alfred Ely Day, "Dog," *The International Standard Bible Encyclopedia*, http://www.bible.org/isbe.asp?id=2765.

MOUNTAINS OF NOTE

Adapted from: Willmington, *Willmington's Book*, 209–11.

NEW TESTAMENT CHURCHES

Adapted from: Willmington, *Willmington's Book*, 53–61.

NON-ISRAELITE KINGS OF THE BIBLE

Adapted from: Willmington, *Willmington's Book*, 179–86.

PROPHETS AND THEIR MESSAGES

Adapted from: Neil S. Wilson and Linda Chaffee Taylor, *Tyndale Handbook of Bible Charts and Maps* (Wheaton, Ill.: Tyndale House, 2001).

QUEENS OF THE BIBLE

Adapted from: Willmington, *Willmington's Book*, 186–187.

SCIENTIFIC ACCURACIES IN THE BIBLE

Adapted from: Willmington, *Willmington's Book,* 306. Matthew J. Slick, "Scientific Accuracies of the Bible," Christian Apologetics and Research Ministry, http://www.carm.org/bible/ms_science.htm.

TOOLS USED TO MAKE DECISIONS

Adapted from: Willmington, *Willmington's Book*, 192-193.

THE TOP 50 MOST MEMORIZED VERSES OF THE BIBLE

Adapted from: Waylon B. Moore, "My Favorite 100 Best Verses to Memorize," *Mentoring,* http://www.mentoring-disciples.org/Best100.html.

THE TWELVE MYTHS OF CHRISTMAS

Adapted from: Paul S. Taylor, "What Are Some of the Most Common Misconceptions about Jesus Christ's Birth?," ChristianAnswers.net, http://www.christiananswers.net/christmas/mythsaboutchristmas.html.

SUBJECT INDEX

ABOUT THE AUTHOR

T.J. McTavish is an amateur church historian, has the world's largest collection of bobble-head dolls, and is hard at work on a Bible study series for women entitled *Word to Your Mother*.